Oster Large Convection Toaster Oven Cookbook for Beginners

1000-Day Amazing Recipes for Delicious and Healthy Meals with Your Convection Toaster Oven

Conry Farkey

Table of Contents

Chapter 1: Breakfast

Egg & Bacon Toast Cups

Preparation Time: 10 minutes
Cooking Time: 20 minutes
Servings: 4

Ingredients:

- Cooking spray
- 2 slices whole-wheat bread, crust trimmed and slice into 2
- 4 strips bacon, cooked crispy
- 4 eggs
- Salt and pepper to taste

Method:

1. Spray your muffin pan with oil.
2. Press bread into the muffin cups.
3. Add the bacon on top of the bread.
4. Crack the egg into each muffin cup.
5. Sprinkle with salt and pepper.
6. Cook in the toaster oven at 350 degrees F for 15 to 20 minutes.

French Toast

Preparation Time: 15 minutes
Cooking Time: 15 minutes
Servings: 4

Ingredients:

- 2 slices bread
- 2 teaspoons sugar
- ½ cup milk
- 2 eggs, beaten

Method:

1. Preheat your toaster oven to 350 degrees F.
2. In a bowl, mix the sugar, milk and eggs.
3. Dip the bread slices into the mixture.
4. Bake in the oven for 6 to 7 minutes per side.

Baked Marinara Eggs

Preparation Time: 15 minutes
Cooking Time: 15 minutes
Servings: 6

Ingredients:

- Butter for greasing
- 6 eggs
- 1 cup marinara sauce
- 1/4 cup all-purpose cream
- 1/4 cup Parmesan cheese, shredded
- Salt and pepper to taste

Method:

1. Grease muffin pan with butter.
2. Preheat your toaster oven to 400 degrees F.
3. Pour marinara into the muffin cups.
4. Crack an egg into each of the muffin cup.
5. Top with cream and cheese.
6. Season with salt and pepper.
7. Bake in the oven for 15 minutes.

Greek Frittata

Preparation Time: 15 minutes
Cooking Time: 30 minutes
Servings: 4

Ingredients:

- 1 tablespoon olive oil
- 10 eggs
- Salt and pepper to taste
- 4 scallions, chopped
- 1-pint cherry tomatoes, sliced in half
- 5 oz. baby spinach, cooked
- 8 oz. feta, crumbled

Method:

1. Preheat your toaster oven to 350 degrees F.
2. Grease casserole dish with olive oil.
3. In a bowl, beat the eggs and season with salt and pepper.
4. Stir in the rest of the ingredients.
5. Pour mixture into the dish.
6. Bake for 30 minutes.

Date Bread

Preparation Time: 15 minutes
Cooking Time: 22 minutes
Servings: 10

Ingredients:

- 2½ cup dates, pitted and chopped
- ¼ cup butter
- 1 cup hot water
- 1½ cups flour
- ½ cup brown sugar
- 1 teaspoon baking powder

- 1 teaspoon baking soda
- ½ teaspoon salt
- 1 egg

Method:

1. In a large bowl, add the dates, butter and top with the hot water.
2. Set aside for about 5 minutes.
3. In a separate bowl, mix together the flour, brown sugar, baking powder, baking soda and salt.
4. In the bowl of dates, add the flour mixture and egg and mix well.
5. Place the mixture into a greased baking pan.
6. Arrange the drip pan in the bottom of Toaster Oven.
7. Place the baking pan over the drip pan.
8. Select "Air Fry" and then adjust the temperature to 340 degrees F.
9. Set the timer for 22 minutes and press "Start".
10. When the display shows "Turn Food" do nothing.
11. When cooking time is complete, remove the pan from Toaster Oven and place the pan onto a wire rack for about 10-15 minutes.
12. Carefully, invert the bread onto the wire rack to cool completely before slicing.
13. Cut the bread into desired size slices and serve.

Spinach Muffins

Preparation Time: 15 minutes
Cooking Time: 10 minutes
Servings: 2

Ingredients:

- 2 large eggs
- 2 tablespoons heavy cream
- 2 tablespoons frozen spinach, thawed
- 4 teaspoons ricotta cheese, crumbled
- Salt and ground black pepper, as required

Method:

1. Grease 2 ramekins.
2. In each prepared ramekin, crack 1 egg.
3. Divide the cream spinach, cheese, salt and black pepper in each ramekin and gently stir to combine, without breaking the yolks.
4. Arrange a sheet pan in the center of Toaster Oven.
5. Place the muffin molds over the sheet pan.
6. Select "Air Fry" and then adjust the temperature to 330 degrees F.
7. Set the timer for 10 minutes and press "Start".
8. When the display shows "Turn Food" do nothing.
9. When cooking time is complete, remove the muffin molds from Toaster Oven and place the pan onto a wire rack for about 10 minutes.
10. Carefully, invert the muffins onto the platter and serve warm.

Blueberry Muffins

Preparation Time: 15 minutes
Cooking Time: 30 minutes
Servings: 4

Ingredients:

- Cooking spray
- 1/2 cup buttermilk
- 1 egg
- 2 tablespoons sugar
- 2 tablespoons applesauce
- 1/3 cup cornmeal
- 2/3 cup whole wheat flour
- 2 teaspoons baking powder
- Pinch salt
- Pinch cinnamon powder
- 1/2 cup blueberries

Method:

1. Spray muffin pan with oil.
2. Preheat your toaster oven to 350 degrees F.

3. In a bowl, combine all the ingredients.
4. Pour mixture into the muffin cups.
5. Bake for 25 to 30 minutes or until fully cooked.

Breakfast Hash

Preparation Time: 5 minutes
Cooking Time: 25 minutes
Serving: 1

Ingredients:

- 2 slices bacon, cooked
- 4 potatoes, sliced and boiled
- 1 egg
- 1/4 cup cheddar cheese, shredded

Method:

1. Add bacon strips to a small baking pan.
2. Top with the potatoes.
3. Crack an egg on top.
4. Bake in the toaster oven at 350 degrees F for 20 minutes.
5. Sprinkle cheese on top and bake for another 5 minutes.

Breakfast Tart

Preparation Time: 15 minutes
Cooking Time: 30 minutes
Servings: 4

Ingredients:

- 1 9 x 13-inch puff pastry sheet
- 1/2 cup cheddar cheese, shredded

- 7 strips bacon, cooked crispy and chopped
- 1/2 cup spinach, cooked
- 4 eggs

Method:

1. Preheat your toaster oven to 400 degrees F.
2. Add the puff pastry sheet to a small pan.
3. Pierce the center with a fork.
4. Bake it for 10 minutes.
5. Take it out of the oven.
6. Sprinkle cheddar cheese on top.
7. Top with the bacon and spinach.
8. Crack eggs in the middle.
9. Bake for 15 minutes.
10. Let cool before serving.

Tofu & Mushroom Omelet

Preparation Time: 15 minutes
Cooking Time: 33 minutes
Servings: 2

Ingredients:

- 2 teaspoons canola oil
- ¼ of onion, chopped
- 1 garlic clove, minced
- 8 ounces silken tofu, drained, pressed and sliced
- 3½ ounces fresh mushrooms, sliced
- Salt and freshly ground black pepper, as needed
- 3 eggs, beaten

Method:

1. In a frying pan, heat the oil over medium heat and sauté the onion and garlic for about 3-4 minutes.
2. Add the mushrooms and cook for about 3-4 minutes.
3. Stir in the mushrooms, salt and black pepper and remove from the heat.
4. Transfer the mixture into a baking dish.
5. Arrange the baking dish in the center of Toaster Oven.
6. Select "Air Fry" and then adjust the temperature to 355 degrees F.
7. Set the timer for 25 minutes and press "Start".
8. When the display shows "Turn Food" stir the mixture.
9. When cooking time is complete, remove the baking dish from Toaster Oven.
10. Cut the omelet into 2 portions and serve hot

Chicken Omelet

Preparation Time: 10 minutes
Cooking Time: 10 minutes
Servings: 2

Ingredients:

- 1 teaspoon olive oil
- 2 scallions, chopped
- ½ jalapeño pepper, seeded and chopped
- 3 eggs
- Salt and ground black pepper, as required
- ¼ cup cooked bacon, chopped

Method:

1. In a frying pan, heat the oil over medium heat and cook the scallion for about 2-3 minutes.
2. Add the jalapeño pepper and cook for about 1 minute.
3. Remove from the heat and set aside to cool slightly.
4. Meanwhile, in a bowl, add the eggs, salt, and black pepper and beat well.
5. Add the scallion mixture and chicken and stir to combine.
6. Place the chicken mixture into a small baking dish.
7. Arrange the baking dish in the center of Toaster Oven.

8. Select "Air Fry" and then adjust the temperature to 355 degrees F.
9. Set the timer for 6 minutes and press "Start".
10. When the display shows "Turn Food" do nothing.
11. When cooking time is complete, remove the baking dish from Toaster Oven.
12. Cut the omelet into 2 portions and serve hot.

Sunny Side Up Eggs

Preparation Time: 5 minutes

Cooking Time: 15 minutes

Serving: 1

Ingredients:

- Cooking spray
- 2 eggs
- Salt and pepper to taste

Method:

1. Spray a small baking pan with oil.
2. Crack 2 eggs into the prepared pan.
3. Bake the eggs for 15 minutes.
4. Season with salt and pepper.

Bacon, Kale & Tomato Frittata

Preparation Time: 15 minutes

Cooking Time: 16 minutes

Servings: 2

Ingredients:

- ¼ cup bacon, chopped

- ¼ cup fresh kale, tough ribs removed and chopped
- ½ of tomato, cubed
- 3 eggs
- Salt and ground black pepper, as required
- ¼ cup Parmesan cheese, grated

Method:

1. Heat a nonstick skillet over medium heat and cook the bacon for about 5 minutes.
2. Add the kale and cook for about 1-2 minutes.
3. Add the tomato and cook for about 2-3 minutes.
4. Remove from the heat and drain the grease from skillet.
5. Set aside to cool slightly.
6. Meanwhile, in a small bowl, add the eggs, salt and black pepper and beat well.
7. In a greased baking dish, place the bacon mixture and top with the eggs, followed by the cheese.
8. Arrange the baking dish in the center of Toaster Oven.
9. Select "Air Fry" and then adjust the temperature to 355 degrees F.
10. Set the timer for 8 minutes and press "Start".
11. When the display shows "Turn Food" do nothing.
12. When cooking time is complete, remove the baking dish from Toaster Oven.
13. Cut into equal-sized wedges and serve.

Baked Eggs & Mushrooms

Preparation Time: 10 minutes
Cooking Time: 15 minutes
Servings: 4

Ingredients:

- 1 tablespoon butter
- 1 onion, chopped
- 1/2 cup mushrooms
- 2 slices ham, chopped
- 1 cup baby spinach
- 4 eggs

- Salt and pepper to taste
- 1 cup mozzarella cheese, grated

Method:

1. Add butter to a pan over medium heat.
2. Cook onion, mushrooms and ham for 3 to 5 minutes, stirring.
3. Stir in spinach.
4. Cook for 2 minutes.
5. Pour mixture into a muffin pan.
6. Crack eggs into each muffin cup.
7. Season with salt and pepper.
8. Bake in the toaster oven at 375 degrees F for 15 minutes.
9. Sprinkle with cheese and bake for another 5 minutes.

Cheesy Egg Toasts

Preparation Time: 10 minutes
Cooking Time: 10 minutes
Servings: 2

Ingredients:

- 4 bread slices
- 4 teaspoons unsalted butter
- Salt and ground black pepper, as required
- 4 eggs
- 4 teaspoon cheddar cheese, shredded

Method:

1. With a butter knife, press the crust edges of each bread slice to create the rectangle.
2. With a teaspoon, gently press the bread down to form the inside of the rectangle without tearing.
3. Season each bread slice with salt and black pepper lightly.

4. Carefully, crack one egg into the center of each bread slice.
5. Season the egg with salt and black pepper.
6. Spread the butter over the edges of each slice. (Avoid to touch the butter to eggs).
7. Now sprinkle the cheese onto the butter.
8. Arrange the bread slices onto a greased cooking tray.
9. Arrange the drip pan in the bottom of Toaster Oven.
10. Insert the cooking tray in the center position.
11. Select "Bake" and then adjust the temperature to 350 degrees F.
12. Set the timer for 10 minutes and press "Start".
13. When the display shows "Add Food" place the baking pan over the drip pan.
14. When the display shows "Turn Food" do nothing.
15. When cooking time is complete, remove the cooking tray from Toaster Oven and serve immediately.

Breakfast Sandwich

Preparation Time: 5 minutes
Cooking Time: 10 minutes
Serving: 1

Ingredients:

- Oil for greasing
- 1 egg
- Salt and pepper to taste
- 1 English muffin, sliced in two
- 1 slice Provolone cheese

Method:

1. Grease a small baking pan with oil.
2. Crack the egg into the pan.
3. Sprinkle with salt and pepper.
4. Bake the egg in the toaster oven until yolk is firm.
5. Toast the muffin until golden.

6. Put the egg on top of the muffin and add the cheese.

Simple Bread

Preparation Time: 15 minutes
Cooking Time: 25 minutes
Servings: 10

Ingredients:

- 2 tablespoons unsalted butter, melted
- 1½ teaspoons active dry yeast
- 1½ teaspoons sugar
- 1½ teaspoons kosher salt
- 2 2/3 cups all-purpose flour

Method:

1. In a stand mixer fitted with the dough hook attachment the butter, yeast, sugar, salt and water and mix on low speed, adding ½ cup of the flour at a time.
2. After adding all the flour, mix on medium speed for about 8 minutes.
3. Place the dough into a 6x3-inch round baking pan.
4. With a plastic wrap, cover the bowl and set aside in room temperature for about 1 hour or until doubled in size.
5. Arrange the drip pan in the bottom of Toaster Oven.
6. Place the baking pan over the drip pan.
7. Select "Bake" and then adjust the temperature to 400 degrees F.
8. Set the timer for 25 minutes and press "Start".
9. When the display shows "Add Food" place the baking pan over the drip pan.
10. When the display shows "Turn Food" rotate the baking pan.
11. When cooking time is complete, remove the pan from Toaster Oven and place the pan onto a wire rack for about 10-15 minutes.
12. Carefully, invert the bread onto the wire rack to cool completely before slicing.
13. Cut the bread into desired size slices and serve.

Pumpkin Bread

Preparation Time: 15 minutes
Cooking Time: 1 hour
Servings: 8

Ingredients:

- 1 cup all-purpose flour
- ½ teaspoon baking soda
- ¼ teaspoon ground cinnamon
- ¼ teaspoon ground nutmeg
- 1/8 teaspoon ground ginger
- 1/8 teaspoon ground cloves
- 1/8 teaspoon salt
- 1 egg
- 1 cup pumpkin puree
- ¾ cup white sugar
- ¼ cup vegetable oil
- ¼ cup walnuts, chopped

Method:

1. In a bowl, add the flour, baking soda, spices and salt and mix well.
2. In another bowl, add the egg, pumpkin puree, sugar and oil and beat until well combined.
3. Slowly, add the flour mixture and mix until well combined.
4. Lightly, dust a small greased loaf pan with flour and gently tap off the excess.
5. Place the mixture into the prepared loaf pan.
6. With a piece of foil, cover the loaf pan.
7. Arrange the drip pan in the bottom of Toaster Oven.
8. Place the loaf pan over the drip pan.
9. Select "Bake" and then adjust the temperature to 350 degrees F.
10. Set the timer for 1 hour and press "Start".
11. When the display shows "Turn Food" rotate the baking pan.
12. When cooking time is complete, remove the pan from Toaster Oven and place the pan onto a wire rack for about 10-15 minutes.
13. Carefully, invert the bread onto the wire rack to cool completely before slicing.
14. Cut the bread into desired size slices and serve.

Oats & Cranberry Muffins

Preparation Time: 15 minutes
Cooking Time: 10 minutes
Servings: 4

Ingredients:

- ½ cup flour
- ¼ cup rolled oats
- 1/8 teaspoon baking powder
- ½ cup powdered sugar
- ½ cup butter, softened
- 2 eggs
- ¼ teaspoon vanilla extract
- ¼ cup dried cranberries

Method:

1. In a bowl, mix together the flour, oats, and baking powder.
2. In another bowl, add the sugar, and butter. Beat until you get the creamy texture.
3. Then, add in the egg and vanilla extract and beat until well combined.
4. Add the egg mixture into oat mixture and mix until just combined.
5. Fold in the cranberries.
6. Place the mixture into 4 greased muffin molds evenly.
7. Arrange a sheet pan in the center of Toaster Oven.
8. Place the muffin molds over the sheet pan.
9. Select "Air Fry" and then adjust the temperature to 355 degrees F.
10. Set the timer for 10 minutes and press "Start".
11. When the display shows "Turn Food" do nothing.
12. When cooking time is complete, remove the muffin molds from Toaster Oven and place the pan onto a wire rack for about 10 minutes.
13. Carefully, invert the muffins onto the wire rack to completely cool before serving.

Tomato Quiche

Preparation Time: 15 minutes

Cooking Time: 30 minutes

Servings: 2

Ingredients:

- 4 eggs
- ¼ cup scallion, chopped
- ½ cup fresh plum tomatoes, chopped
- ½ cup unsweetened almond milk
- 1 cup Cheddar cheese, shredded
- Salt and freshly ground black pepper, as required

Method:

1. In a small baking dish, add all the ingredients and mix well.
2. Arrange the baking dish in the center of Toaster Oven.
3. Select "Air Fry" and then adjust the temperature to 340 degrees F.
4. Set the timer for 30 minutes and press "Start".
5. When the display shows "Turn Food" do nothing.
6. When cooking time is complete, remove the baking dish from Toaster Oven.
7. Cut into equal-sized wedges and serve.

Chapter 2: Meat

Glazed Pork Tenderloin

Preparation Time: 15 minutes

Cooking Time: 40 minutes

Servings: 4

Ingredients:

- Cooking spray
- 1 lb. pork tenderloin strips
- 1 teaspoon steak seasoning blend
- 1 onion, sliced into wedges
- 2 parsnips, sliced
- 2 carrots, sliced
- 1 tablespoon olive oil
- Salt and pepper to taste
- 1 tablespoon balsamic vinegar
- 1/2 cup apricot jam

Method:

1. Preheat your toaster oven to 425 degrees F.
2. Spray your baking pan with oil.
3. Season pork strips with seasoning blend.
4. Place pork strips in the middle of the pan.
5. In a bowl, toss onion, parsnips and carrots in olive oil.
6. Season with salt and pepper.
7. Add the vegetables around the pork tenderloin.
8. Bake in the toaster for 30 minutes.
9. Mix vinegar and apricot jam.
10. Drizzle mixture over the pork and veggies.
11. Bake for another 10 minutes.
12. Let cool and serve.

Meatballs

Preparation Time: 10 minutes
Cooking Time: 35 minutes
Servings:4

Ingredients:

- 1 lb ground beef
- 1/3 cup milk
- 2 jalapenos, minced
- 4 oz cream cheese
- 1 tsp dried basil
- 2 tbsp Worcestershire sauce
- 1/2 cup cheddar cheese, shredded
- 3/4 cup breadcrumbs
- 1/2 onion, minced
- 1 tsp salt

Method:

1. Add all ingredients into the bowl and mix until well combined.
2. Make balls from the meat mixture and place on mesh rack then insert rack into the toaster oven.
3. Set the temperature to 400 F and timer for 35 minutes. Press start.
4. Serve and enjoy.

Broiled Steak

Preparation Time: 15 minutes
Cooking Time: 30 minutes
Servings: 2

Ingredients:

- 1/4 cup butter
- 1/2 teaspoon mustard
- 1 tablespoon Worcestershire sauce
- Salt and pepper to taste
- 1/2 lb. steak strips

Method:

1. Set your toaster oven to broil.
2. In a bowl, mix the butter, mustard and Worcestershire sauce.
3. Sprinkle both sides of steak with salt and pepper.
4. Coat with the butter mixture.
5. Broil in the toaster oven for 15 minutes.
6. Brush both sides and flip.
7. Broil for another 15 minutes.

Cajun Pork Chops

Preparation Time: 40 minutes
Cooking Time: 40 minutes
Servings: 4

Ingredients:

- Cooking spray
- 4 pork chops
- Salt and pepper to taste
- 1 1/2 teaspoons paprika
- 1 1/2 teaspoons garlic powder
- 1 teaspoon dried thyme
- 1 teaspoon cayenne pepper

Method:

1. Preheat toaster oven to 375 degrees F.
2. Spray baking pan with oil.
3. Season pork chops with a mixture of salt, pepper, herbs and spices.
4. Bake pork chops for 40 minutes in the toaster oven, flipping once.

Baked Pork Chops

Preparation Time: 15 minutes
Cooking Time: 30 minutes
Servings: 4

Ingredients:

- Cooking spray
- 2 tablespoons brown sugar
- 1/4 teaspoon onion powder
- 1/2 teaspoon garlic powder
- 1/2 teaspoon chili powder
- Salt and pepper to taste
- 4 pork chops
- 3 tablespoons olive oil

Method:

1. Preheat your toaster oven to 400 degrees F.
2. Spray your baking pan with oil.
3. In a bowl, mix the sugar, onion powder, garlic powder, chili powder, salt and pepper.
4. Brush both sides of pork with olive oil.
5. Sprinkle with sugar mixture.
6. Bake in the toaster oven for 20 to 30 minutes.

Creole Chops

Preparation Time: 10 minutes
Cooking Time: 12 minutes
Servings: 6

Ingredients:

- 1 1/2 lbs pork chops, boneless
- 1 tsp paprika
- 1 tsp Creole seasoning
- 1 tsp garlic powder

- 1/4 cup parmesan cheese, grated
- 1/3 cup almond flour

Method:

1. Add all ingredients except pork chops into the zip-lock bag.
2. Add pork chops into the bag. Seal bag and shake well.
3. Remove pork chops from the zip-lock bag and place on mesh rack then insert rack into the toaster oven.
4. Select air fry mode then set the temperature to 360 F and timer for 12 minutes. Press start.
5. Serve and enjoy.

Meatballs

Preparation Time: 10 minutes
Cooking Time: 20 minutes
Servings: 4

Ingredients:

- 1 egg, lightly beaten
- 1 lb ground lamb
- 1 tbsp garlic, minced
- 1/4 tsp pepper
- 1/4 tsp red pepper flakes
- 1 tsp ground cumin
- 2 tsp fresh oregano, chopped
- 2 tbsp fresh parsley, chopped
- 1 tsp kosher salt

Method:

1. Add all ingredients into the mixing bowl and mix until well combined.
2. Make balls from the meat mixture and place on mesh rack then insert rack into the toaster oven.
3. Set the temperature to 400 F and timer for 20-25 minutes. Press start.
4. Serve and enjoy.

Char Siu Pork

Preparation Time: 1 hour and 10 minutes
Cooking Time: 1 hour and 10 minutes
Servings: 4

Ingredients:

- 2 tablespoons soy sauce
- 1 tablespoon sugar
- 1 tablespoon red wine
- 1 tablespoon honey
- ¼ teaspoon Chinese five spice powder
- 1 teaspoon oyster sauce
- 1 teaspoon ginger, grated
- 1 lb. pork shoulder, sliced into cubes

Method:

1. Combine all ingredients in a bowl except pork.
2. Mix well.
3. Reserve 3 tablespoons of this mixture for basting.
4. Marinate pork in the remaining mixture for 1 hour.
5. Cook the pork in the toaster oven at 450 degrees F for 40 minutes.
6. Brush with the sauce.
7. Flip and cook for another 30 minutes.

Meatloaf

Preparation Time: 30 minutes
Cooking Time: 1 hour
Servings: 4

Ingredients:

- 1 1/2 lb. ground beef
- 1 1/2 lb. ground pork
- 2 onions, chopped
- 5 cloves garlic, chopped
- 1/2 cup milk
- 4 tablespoons breadcrumbs
- 1 cup fresh parsley, chopped
- 2 eggs, beaten
- Salt and pepper to taste

Method:

1. Preheat toaster oven to 350 degrees F.
2. Combine all the ingredients in a bowl.
3. Press mixture into a loaf pan.
4. Bake for 1 hour.

Lamb Cutlets

Preparation Time: 10 minutes
Cooking Time: 30 minutes
Servings: 4

Ingredients:

- 4 lamb cutlets
- 1 tsp olive oil
- 1/2 tbsp chives, chopped
- 2 tbsp mustard
- 2 garlic cloves, minced
- 1/2 tbsp oregano, chopped
- 1/2 tbsp basil, chopped
- Pepper
- Salt

Method:

1. Add lamb cutlets and remaining ingredients to the mixing bowl and coat well.
2. Place lamb cutlets on mesh rack then insert rack into the toaster oven.
3. Select air fry mode then set the temperature to 380 F and timer for 30 minutes. Press start. Flip lamb cutlets halfway through.
4. Serve and enjoy.

Grilled Pork Belly

Preparation Time: 3 hours and 10 minutes
Cooking Time: 50 minutes
Servings: 6

Ingredients:

- 1 tablespoon lemon juice
- 1/2 cup soy sauce
- 1/2 cup ketchup
- 1 tablespoon garlic, minced
- Pepper to taste
- 3 lb. pork belly

Method:

1. Mix lemon juice, soy sauce, ketchup, garlic and pepper in a bowl.
2. Marinate the pork belly in the mixture for at least 3 hours, covered in the refrigerator.
3. Preheat toaster oven to 375 degrees F.
4. Put a grill rack inside the toaster oven.
5. Add the pork belly to the grill rack.
6. Cook for 20 minutes.
7. Flip and cook another 20 minutes.
8. Increase temperature to 450 degrees F.
9. Cook for 10 minutes.

Beef Fajitas

Preparation Time: 10 minutes
Cooking Time: 8 minutes
Servings: 4

Ingredients:

- 1 lb steak, sliced
- 1 tsp cumin
- 1 yellow bell peppers, sliced
- 1/2 tbsp chili powder
- 3 tbsp olive oil
- 1 green bell peppers, sliced
- 1 tsp garlic powder
- 1 tsp smoked paprika
- Pepper
- Salt

Method:

1. In a large bowl, toss sliced steak with remaining ingredients and spread on mesh rack then insert rack into the toaster oven.
2. Select air fry mode then set the temperature to 390 F and timer for 8 minutes. Press start.
3. Serve and enjoy.

Easy Ranch Pork Chops

Preparation Time: 10 minutes
Cooking Time: 35 minutes
Servings: 6

Ingredients:

- 6 pork chops, boneless
- 2 tbsp olive oil
- 1 oz ranch seasoning

Method:

1. Mix oil and ranch seasoning and rub over pork chops.
2. Place pork chops on mesh rack then insert rack into the toaster oven.
3. Select air fry mode then set the temperature to 400 F and timer for 35 minutes. Press start. Turn pork chops halfway through.
4. Serve and enjoy.

Herbed Beef Tenderloin

Preparation Time: 30 minutes
Cooking Time: 40 minutes
Servings: 6

Ingredients:

- 1 1/2 lb. beef tenderloin, sliced into strips
- Salt and pepper to taste
- 2 tablespoons mustard
- 3 cloves garlic
- 1 tablespoon fresh oregano, chopped
- 2 tablespoons fresh rosemary, chopped
- 2 tablespoons fresh thyme, chopped
- 1 teaspoon dried tarragon
- 3 tablespoons olive oil

Method:

1. Preheat your toaster oven to 375 degrees F.
2. Season beef with salt and pepper.
3. Rub it with mustard.
4. Add the remaining ingredients to a food processor.
5. Pulse until smooth.
6. Cover the steak strips with the herb mixture.
7. Bake in the toaster oven for 40 minutes.

Garlic Lemon Lamb Chops

Preparation Time: 10 minutes
Cooking Time: 6 minutes
Servings: 6

Ingredients:

- 6 lamb loin chops
- 1 tbsp dried rosemary
- 1 tbsp olive oil
- 1 tbsp garlic, minced
- 2 tbsp fresh lemon juice
- 1 ½ tbsp lemon zest
- Pepper
- Salt

Method:

1. Add lamb chops in a mixing bowl.
2. Add remaining ingredients on top of lamb chops and coat well.
3. Arrange lamb chops on mesh rack then insert rack into the toaster oven.
4. Select air fry mode then set the temperature to 400 F and timer for 6 minutes. Press start.
5. Serve and enjoy.

Garlic Herb Pork

Preparation Time: 15 minutes
Cooking Time: 35 minutes
Servings: 4

Ingredients:

- 3 cloves garlic
- 1 tablespoon fresh rosemary, chopped
- 1 tablespoon fresh parsley, chopped
- 1/2 tablespoon fresh thyme, chopped
- 2 tablespoons olive oil
- Salt to taste
- 4 pork chops

Method:

1. Preheat toaster oven to 450 degrees F.
2. Add garlic, herbs, oil and salt in a food processor.
3. Pulse until smooth.
4. Coat pork chops with this mixture.

5. Broil in the toaster oven for 15 to 20 minutes.
6. Flip and broil for another 15 minutes.

Cheesesteak Sandwich

Preparation Time: 30 minutes
Cooking Time: 4 hours and 15 minutes
Servings: 4

Ingredients:

- 2 lb. beef strips
- 2 green bell peppers, sliced into strips
- 2 onions, sliced
- Salt to taste
- 4 tablespoons Italian salad dressing
- 1 cup beef stock
- 4 hoagie rolls, sliced into 2
- 4 slices cheddar cheese

Method:

1. Add the beef strips, onion and green bell peppers to a slow cooker.
2. Pour in beef stock.
3. Season with salt and Italian salad dressing.
4. Cook on low for 4 hours.
5. Set toaster oven to high.
6. Add the rolls to a baking pan.
7. Top the rolls with the beef mixture.
8. Place cheese slices on top.
9. Toast for 5 minutes.

Healthy & Juicy Pork Chops

Preparation Time: 5 minutes

Cooking Time: 16 minutes

Servings: 4

Ingredients:

- 4 pork chops, boneless
- 1/2 tsp onion powder
- 1/2 tsp garlic powder
- 1/4 tsp sugar
- 2 tsp olive oil
- 1/2 tsp celery seed
- 1/2 tsp parsley
- 1/2 tsp salt

Method:

1. In a small bowl, mix sugar, garlic powder, onion powder, parsley, celery seed, and salt.
2. Rub oil and seasoning on the pork chops.
3. Place pork chops on mesh rack then insert rack into the toaster oven.
4. Set the temperature to 350 F and timer for 16 minutes. Press start.
5. Serve and enjoy.

BBQ Pork Chops

Preparation Time: 10 minutes

Cooking Time: 14 minutes

Servings 2

Ingredients:

- 2 pork chops
- 1/4 cup BBQ sauce
- 1 tsp garlic, minced
- 1/2 tsp olive oil
- Pepper
- Salt

Method:

1. Add all ingredients into the bowl and mix well and place in the refrigerator for 1 hour.
2. Place marinated pork chops on mesh rack then insert rack into the toaster oven.

3. Select air fry mode then set the temperature to 350 F and timer for 14 minutes. Press start. Turn pork chops halfway through.
4. Serve and enjoy.

Healthy Beef Patties

Preparation Time: 10 minutes
Cooking Time: 35 minutes
Servings: 6

Ingredients:

- 1 lb ground beef
- 2 eggs, lightly beaten
- 1/2 tsp chili powder
- 1 tsp curry powder
- 1 cup breadcrumbs
- 1/2 onion, chopped
- 2 medium zucchini, grated
- Pepper
- Salt

Method:

1. Add all ingredients into the large bowl and mix until well combined.
2. Make patties from meat mixture and place on mesh rack then insert rack into the toaster oven.
3. Set the temperature to 400 F and timer for 35 minutes. Press start.
4. Serve and enjoy.

Chapter 3: Poultry

Shredded Chicken

Preparation Time: 15 minutes

Cooking Time: 15 minutes

Servings: 2

Ingredients:

- 1/4 cup chicken, cooked and shredded
- 2 tablespoons garlic mayo sauce
- 2 tortillas
- 1/4 cup cheddar cheese, shredded
- 2 teaspoons Parmesan cheese

Method:

1. Mix shredded chicken and garlic mayo sauce in a bowl.
2. Top tortillas with this mixture.
3. Sprinkle cheddar and Parmesan cheese on top.
4. Roll up the tortillas.
5. Toast in the toaster oven for 15 minutes.

Lemon Garlic Chicken

Preparation Time: 10 minutes

Cooking Time: 30 minutes

Servings: 4

Ingredients:

- 1 lb chicken drumsticks
- 4 garlic cloves, minced

- 1 tbsp olive oil
- 1 tbsp parsley, minced
- 1/2 fresh lemon juice
- Pepper
- Salt

Method:

1. Season chicken with pepper and salt.
2. Mix together parsley, lemon juice, garlic, and oil and rub over chicken.
3. Place chicken drumsticks on mesh rack then insert rack into the toaster oven.
4. Set the temperature to 380 F and timer for 30 minutes. Press start. Turn chicken halfway through.
5. Serve and enjoy.

Baked Chicken Strips

Preparation Time: 15 minutes

Cooking Time: 20 minutes

Servings: 6

Ingredients:

- 2 teaspoons melted butter
- 2/3 cup breadcrumbs
- 2/3 cup crackers, crushed
- 2 eggs
- Salt and pepper to taste
- 1 1/2 lb. chicken strips

Method:

1. Preheat toaster oven to 450 degrees F.
2. Spray small baking pan with oil.
3. In a bowl, mix butter, breadcrumbs and crushed crackers.
4. In another bowl, beat the eggs and season with salt and pepper.
5. Dip chicken strip in egg mixture and then in butter mixture.
6. Arrange in a single layer in the baking pan.

7. Bake for 10 minutes per side.

Chicken Casserole

Preparation Time: 30 minutes
Cooking Time: 30 minutes
Servings: 4

Ingredients:

- 4 cups chicken, cooked and sliced into cubes
- 2 cups cheddar cheese soup
- 3 cups spinach, chopped
- 1 cup light mayonnaise
- 1 cup milk
- 4 cups cooked pasta
- 2 cups Monterey Jack cheese, shredded
- 1 cup bacon, cooked crispy and chopped

Method:

1. Preheat your oven to 375 degrees F.
2. In a bowl, mix chicken, cheddar soup, spinach, mayo and milk.
3. Add pasta to a baking pan.
4. Pour chicken mixture on top.
5. Bake in the toaster oven for 20 minutes.
6. Sprinkle cheese and bacon on top.
7. Bake for another 10 minutes.

Spicy Chicken Wings

Preparation Time: 10 minutes
Cooking Time: 30 minutes

Servings: 4

Ingredients:

- 2 lbs chicken wings
- ½ tsp smoked paprika
- 2 tsp garlic powder
- 4 tsp chili powder
- 3 tbsp olive oil
- Pepper
- Salt

Method:

1. Add chicken wings and remaining ingredients into the zip-lock bag and shake well to coat.
2. Place chicken wings on mesh rack then insert rack into the toaster oven.
3. Select air fry mode then set the temperature to 380 F and timer for 30 minutes. Press start. Turn chicken wings halfway through.
4. Serve and enjoy.

Baked Crispy Chicken

Preparation Time: 15 minutes
Cooking Time: 1 hour
Servings: 6

Ingredients:

- 2 lb. chicken
- Vegetable oil
- Salt and pepper to taste
- 2 tablespoons flour
- 1/4 cup water

Method:

1. Coat chicken with oil.
2. Season with salt and pepper.
3. Dredge with flour.

4. Cook in the toaster oven at 400 degrees F for 1 hour.

Chicken & Veggies with Rosemary

Preparation Time: 20 minutes
Cooking Time: 1 hour and 10 minutes
Servings: 4

Ingredients:

- 3 sprigs rosemary
- 1 onion, sliced into wedges
- 2 cloves garlic, peeled
- 1 sweet potato, sliced into cubes
- 1 parsnip, sliced into cubes
- 1 turnip, sliced into cubes
- 2 tablespoons olive oil
- Salt and pepper to taste
- 1/2 teaspoon garlic powder
- 4 chicken thighs

Method:

1. Preheat toaster oven to 425 degrees F.
2. Spray small baking pan with oil.
3. Put the rosemary in the pan.
4. In a bowl, toss the onion, garlic, sweet potato, parsnip and turnip in oil, salt and pepper.
5. Place veggies in the baking pan.
6. Bake in the toaster oven for 30 minutes.
7. Season chicken with salt, pepper and garlic powder.
8. Add chicken on top of vegetables. Bake for 40 minutes.

Cajun Chicken

Preparation Time: 10 minutes

Cooking Time: 15 minutes

Servings: 4

Ingredients:

- 4 chicken thighs, boneless
- 1 tsp paprika
- 3 tbsp parmesan cheese, grated
- 1/3 cup almond flour
- 1/2 tsp cajun seasoning
- 1 tsp dried mixed herbs

Method:

1. In a medium bowl, mix together almond flour, parmesan cheese, paprika, dried mixed herbs, and Cajun seasoning.
2. Spray chicken thighs with cooking spray and coat with almond flour mixture.
3. Place coated chicken thighs on mesh rack then insert rack into the toaster oven.
4. Select air fry mode then set the temperature to 400 F and timer for 15 minutes. Press start. Turn chicken halfway through.
5. Serve and enjoy.

Garlic Chicken

Preparation Time: 4 hours and 15 minutes

Cooking Time: 20 minutes

Servings: 2

Ingredients:

- 1 tablespoon honey
- 1 tablespoon soy sauce
- 1 teaspoon sesame oil
- 2 chicken breast fillets
- Vegetable oil
- 1 teaspoon garlic powder
- 1 teaspoon dried oregano
- Salt and pepper to taste

Method:

1. Mix honey, soy sauce and sesame oil in a bowl.

2. Marinate the chicken in this mixture for 1 hour.
3. Grease a baking pan with oil.
4. Sprinkle chicken with garlic powder, oregano, salt and pepper.
5. Cook chicken in the toaster oven for 10 minutes per side.

Meatballs

Preparation Time: 10 minutes
Cooking Time: 10 minutes
Servings: 4

Ingredients:

- 1 lb ground chicken
- 2 tbsp parmesan cheese, grated
- 1/4 cup sun-dried tomatoes, drained
- 2 tsp garlic, minced
- 3/4 cup almond flour
- 1/4 cup feta cheese, crumbled
- 3 cups baby spinach
- Pepper
- Salt

Method:

1. Add spinach, sun-dried tomatoes, and 1 tsp garlic into the food processor and process until a paste is formed.
2. Add spinach mixture into the large mixing bowl. Add remaining ingredients into the bowl and mix until well combined.
3. Make balls from mixture and place on mesh rack then insert rack into the toaster oven.
4. Select air fry mode then set the temperature to 400 F and timer for 10 minutes. Press start.
5. Serve and enjoy.

Chicken Meatballs

Preparation Time: 10 minutes
Cooking Time: 12 minutes
Servings: 4

Ingredients:

- 1 egg, lightly beaten
- 1/2 lb ground chicken
- 2 garlic cloves, minced
- 1/2 cup swiss cheese, shredded
- 1/3 cup onion, diced
- 1/2 lb ham, diced
- Pepper
- Salt

Method:

1. Add all ingredients into the mixing bowl and mix until well combined. Place in refrigerator for 30 minutes.
2. Make balls from mixture and place on mesh rack then insert rack into the toaster oven.
3. Select air fry mode then set the temperature to 390 F and timer for 12 minutes. Press start.
4. Serve and enjoy.

Baked Chicken Taters

Preparation Time: 15 minutes
Cooking Time: 35 minutes
Servings: 2

Ingredients:

- 1/2 cup milk
- 1/4 cup butter, sliced into cubes
- 2 cans cream of chicken soup
- 1 cup cheddar cheese, shredded
- 3 cups chicken, cooked and sliced into cubes

- 16 oz. frozen carrots and peas
- 32 oz. tater tots

Method:

1. In a pan over medium heat, mix milk, butter and soup.
2. Cook for 1 minute.
3. Stir in the cheese, chicken and vegetables.
4. Pour mixture into a baking pan.
5. Sprinkle tater tots on top.
6. Cook in the toaster oven at 400 degrees F for 30 minutes.

Meatballs

Preparation Time: 10 minutes
Cooking Time: 10 minutes
Servings: 4

Ingredients:

- 1 egg, lightly beaten
- 1 bell pepper, chopped
- 1 1/2 lbs ground turkey
- 1 tbsp fresh cilantro, minced
- 4 tbsp fresh parsley, chopped
- Pepper
- Salt

Method:

1. Add all ingredients into the mixing bowl and mix until well combined.
2. Make balls from mixture and place on mesh rack then insert rack into the toaster oven.
3. Select air fry mode then set the temperature to 400 F and timer for 10 minutes. Press start.
4. Serve and enjoy.

Cordon Bleu

Preparation Time: 15 minutes
Cooking Time: 20 minutes
Servings: 2

Ingredients:

- 2 chicken breast fillets
- 2 slices cheese
- 2 ham slices
- 1/2 cup all-purpose flour
- Salt and pepper to taste
- Pinch of paprika

- 1 egg
- 2 tablespoons milk
- 1/2 cup breadcrumbs
- 1 tablespoon canola oil
- 1 tablespoon melted butter

Method:

1. Flatten chicken breast with a meat mallet.
2. Top each chicken breast fillet with cheese and ham.
3. Roll up the chicken.
4. Mix flour, salt, pepper and paprika in a bowl.
5. In another bowl, beat egg. Stir in milk.
6. Add breadcrumbs to a third bowl.
7. Dip the chicken in the first, second and third bowls.
8. Coat with oil.
9. Bake in the toaster oven for 20 minutes.
10. Let cool before slicing and serving.

Herb Chicken Wings

Preparation Time: 10 minutes
Cooking Time: 15 minutes

Servings: 4

Ingredients:

- 2 lbs chicken wings
- 1/2 cup parmesan cheese, grated
- 1 tsp Herb de Provence
- 1 tsp smoked paprika
- Pepper
- Salt

Method:

1. Add cheese, paprika, herb de Provence, pepper, and salt into the large mixing bowl. Add chicken wings into the bowl and toss well to coat.
2. Place chicken wings on mesh rack then insert rack into the toaster oven.
3. Select air fry mode then set the temperature to 350 F and timer for 15 minutes. Press start. Turn chicken wings halfway through.
4. Serve and enjoy.

Turkey Meatloaf

Preparation Time: 15 minutes
Cooking Time: 1 hour
Servings: 10

Ingredients:

- 2 lb. lean ground turkey
- 1 onion, chopped
- 1/2 cup carrot, shredded
- 1 cup quick-cooking oats
- 1/2 cup milk
- 1 teaspoon garlic powder
- 1/4 teaspoon pepper
- 2 tablespoons ketchup
- 1 egg

Method:

1. Preheat your oven to 350 degrees F.

2. Combine all the ingredients in a bowl.

3. Press mixture into a loaf pan.

4. Bake in the oven for 1 hour.

Parmesan Chicken

Preparation Time: 20 minutes

Cooking Time: 20 minutes

Servings: 2

Ingredients:

- 2 chicken breast fillets
- Salt and pepper to taste
- 1 egg, beaten
- 3 tablespoons Parmesan cheese
- 1/2 cup breadcrumbs
- Pinch of paprika

- Vegetable oil
- 3 cloves garlic, minced
- 2 tomatoes, chopped
- 1/4 cup tomato paste
- 5 tablespoons mozzarella, shredded

Method:

1. Season chicken breast fillets with salt and pepper.

2. Add egg to a bowl.

3. In another bowl, mix Parmesan cheese, breadcrumbs and paprika.

4. Dip chicken in egg and then in Parmesan cheese mixture.

5. In a pan over medium heat, pour the oil and cook chicken until golden.

6. Transfer to a plate.

7. Pour oil into another bowl.

8. Cook garlic and tomatoes in the same pan.

9. Add tomato paste.

10. Cook for 2 minutes.

11. Spread tomato paste mixture in a small baking pan.
12. Place chicken on top.
13. Sprinkle with mozzarella cheese.
14. Bake in the toaster oven for 10 minutes.

Crispy Chicken

Preparation Time: 10 minutes
Cooking Time: 14 minutes
Servings: 2

Ingredients:

- 2 chicken breasts, boneless and skinless
- 2 cups crushed crackers
- 1 tbsp olive oil
- Pepper
- Salt

Method:

1. Season chicken with pepper and salt.
2. Brush chicken with oil and coat with crushed crackers.
3. Place chicken on mesh rack then insert rack into the toaster oven.
4. Set the temperature to 370 F and timer for 14 minutes. Press start. Turn chicken halfway through.
5. Serve and enjoy.

Turkey Patties

Preparation Time: 10 minutes
Cooking Time: 20 minutes
Servings: 4

Ingredients:

- 1 lb ground turkey
- 1 tbsp olive oil
- 1 tbsp garlic, minced
- 4 oz feta cheese, crumbled
- 1 1/2 cups fresh spinach, chopped
- 1 tsp Italian seasoning
- Pepper
- Salt

Method:

1. Add ground turkey and remaining ingredients into the mixing bowl and mix until well combined.
2. Make four patties from the turkey mixture and place on mesh rack then insert rack into the toaster oven.
3. Set the temperature to 400 F and timer for 20 minutes. Press start.
4. Serve and enjoy.

Perfect Chicken Tenders

Preparation Time: 10 minutes
Cooking Time: 13 minutes
Servings: 4

Ingredients:

- 6 chicken tenders
- 1 tsp paprika
- 1 tsp onion powder
- 1 tsp oregano
- 1 tsp garlic powder
- 1 tsp kosher salt

Method:

1. In a small bowl, mix together onion powder, oregano, garlic powder, paprika, and salt and rub all over chicken tenders.
2. Spray chicken tenders with cooking spray.
3. Place chicken tenders on mesh rack then insert rack into the toaster oven.
4. Select air fry mode then set the temperature to 380 F and timer for 13 minutes. Press start. Turn chicken halfway through.
5. Serve and enjoy.

Chapter 4: Seafood

Walnut-Crusted Salmon

Preparation Time: 15 minutes
Cooking Time: 15 minutes
Servings: 2

Ingredients:

- 2 salmon fillets
- Salt and pepper to taste
- 3 tablespoons walnuts, chopped
- 2 tablespoons olive oil

Method:

1. Preheat your toaster oven to 400 degrees F.
2. Add salmon to a baking pan.
3. Season with salt and pepper.
4. Press walnuts onto the fish.
5. Brush with oil.
6. Bake in the toaster oven for 15 minutes.

Baked Cheesy Salmon

Preparation Time: 20 minutes
Cooking Time: 25 minutes
Servings: 2

Ingredients:

- 2 salmon fillets
- 1 tablespoon lemon juice

- Salt and pepper to taste
- 4 cloves garlic, minced
- 1/4 cup mayonnaise
- 1 teaspoon sugar
- 1 teaspoon liquid seasoning
- 1/4 cup mozzarella cheese, grated

Method:

1. Preheat toaster oven to 400 degrees F.
2. Brush both sides of salmon with lemon juice.
3. Sprinkle with salt, pepper and garlic.
4. Place in a baking pan.
5. In a bowl, mix the remaining ingredients except cheese.
6. Spread mixture on top of salmon.
7. Bake for 15 minutes.
8. Top with cheese.
9. Bake for 10 minutes.

Mustard Salmon with Green Beans

Preparation Time: 30 minutes
Cooking Time: 15 minutes
Servings: 2

Ingredients:

- 2 salmon fillets
- 2 tablespoons olive oil
- 2 cloves garlic
- 1 tablespoon Dijon mustard
- 1 tablespoon soy sauce
- 1 yellow bell pepper, sliced into strips
- 1 red bell pepper, sliced into strips
- 1 leek, chopped
- 6 oz. green beans, trimmed
- Pepper to taste

Method:

1. Preheat toaster oven to 400 degrees F.
2. Spray baking pan with oil.
3. Add salmon to the pan.
4. Combine olive oil, garlic, mustard and soy sauce in a food processor.
5. Pulse until smooth.
6. In a bowl, toss the bell peppers, leeks and green beans in 1 tablespoon of mustard mixture.
7. Add to the pan beside the salmon.
8. Pour remaining mustard mixture on top of salmon.
9. Season with pepper.
10. Bake for 15 minutes.

Cajun Shrimp

Preparation Time: 10 minutes
Cooking Time: 6 minutes
Servings: 2

Ingredients:

- 1/2 lb shrimp, peeled and deveined
- 1/2 tsp old bay seasoning
- 1/2 tsp cayenne pepper
- 1 tbsp olive oil
- 1/4 tsp paprika
- Pinch of salt

Method:

1. Add shrimp and remaining ingredients into the mixing bowl and toss well to coat.
2. Add shrimp on mesh rack then insert rack into the toaster oven.
3. Select air fry mode then set the temperature to 390 F and timer for 6 minutes. Press start.
4. Serve and enjoy.

Miso-Glazed Salmon

Preparation Time: 45 minutes

Cooking Time: 20 minutes

Servings: 4

Ingredients:

- 4 salmon fillets
- 1 tablespoon soy sauce
- 1/4 cup red wine
- 1/4 cup miso
- 1/4 cup sugar
- 2 tablespoons vegetable oil

Method:

1. Dry salmon with paper towels.
2. In a bowl, combine the rest of the ingredients.
3. Add salmon to the bowl.
4. Cover and marinate for 30 minutes.
5. Transfer to a small baking pan.
6. Preheat your toaster oven to 400 degrees F.
7. Set it to broil.
8. Cook for 15 to 20 minutes.

Lemon Butter Shrimp

Preparation Time: 15 minutes

Cooking Time: 25 minutes

Servings: 4

Ingredients:

- Cooking spray

- 1 1/2 lb. shrimp, peeled and deveined
- 1 teaspoon garlic powder
- 1/4 cup butter, melted
- 1/4 cup lemon juice

Method:

1. Preheat toaster oven to 450 degrees F.
2. Spray a small baking pan with oil.
3. Season shrimp with garlic powder.
4. Add to a baking pan.
5. Bake in the toaster oven for 15 minutes.
6. Mix butter and lemon juice in a bowl.
7. Pour mixture over the shrimp and bake for 10 minutes.

Broiled Tilapia with Avocado

Preparation Time: 15 minutes
Cooking Time: 15 minutes
Servings: 2

Ingredients:

- 3 tablespoons sour cream
- 1 avocado, sliced in half and pitted
- 1 teaspoon lime juice
- 2 tilapia fillets
- 1 tablespoon mayonnaise
- Garlic salt

Method:

1. Add sour cream, avocado and lime juice to a food processor.
2. Pulse until smooth.
3. Transfer to a bowl.
4. Cover the bowl and refrigerate.

5. Spread fish fillet with mayo.
6. Sprinkle both sides with garlic salt.
7. Place in a baking pan.
8. Set your toaster oven to broil.
9. Broil for 10 to 15 minutes.
10. Serve with avocado and lime sauce.

Chipotle Shrimp

Preparation Time: 10 minutes
Cooking Time: 8 minutes
Servings: 4

Ingredients:

- 1 1/2 lbs shrimp, peeled and deveined
- 1 /4 tsp ground cumin
- 2 tsp chipotle in adobo
- 2 tbsp olive oil
- 4 tbsp lime juice

Method:

1. Add shrimp, oil, lime juice, cumin, and chipotle in a zip-lock bag. Seal bag shake well and place it in the refrigerator for 30 minutes.
2. Thread marinated shrimp onto skewers and place on mesh rack then insert rack into the toaster oven.
3. Select air fry mode then set the temperature to 350 F and timer for 8 minutes. Press start.
4. Serve and enjoy.

Pesto Salmon

Preparation Time: 15 minutes

Cooking Time: 15 minutes

Servings: 4

Ingredients:

- Cooking spray
- 4 salmon fillets
- 2 tablespoons white wine
- 2 tablespoons pesto
- 2 tablespoons pine nuts

Method:

1. Spray your baking pan with oil.
2. Add salmon fillet to the pan.
3. Drizzle with white wine.
4. Spread pesto and sprinkle with pine nuts.
5. Cook in the toaster oven at 400 degrees F for 15 minutes.

Shrimp Fajitas

Preparation Time: 10 minutes
Cooking Time: 22 minutes
Servings: 12

Ingredients:

- 1 lb shrimp, tail-off
- 1 red bell pepper, diced
- 2 tbsp taco seasoning
- 1/2 cup onion, diced
- 1 green bell pepper, diced

Method:

1. Add shrimp, taco seasoning, onion, and bell peppers into the mixing bowl and toss well.
2. Place shrimp mixture on mesh rack then insert rack into the toaster oven.

3. Select air fry mode then set the temperature to 390 F and timer for 22 minutes. Press start. Stir halfway through.
4. Serve and enjoy.

Parmesan Fish Fillets

Preparation Time: 10 minutes
Cooking Time: 15 minutes
Servings: 4

Ingredients:

- 4 cod fillets
- 2 tsp paprika
- 3/4 cup parmesan cheese, grated
- 1 tbsp olive oil
- 1 tbsp parsley, chopped
- 1/4 tsp sea salt

Method:

1. In a shallow dish, mix together parmesan cheese, paprika, parsley, and salt.
2. Brush fish fillets with oil and coat with cheese mixture.
3. Place fish fillets on mesh rack then insert rack into the toaster oven.
4. Set the temperature to 400 F and timer for 15 minutes. Press start.
5. Serve and enjoy.

Parmesan Fish Fillet

Preparation Time: 15 minutes
Cooking Time: 15 minutes
Servings: 2

Ingredients:

- 2 oz. Parmesan cheese, grated
- 1/4 cup breadcrumbs
- Pepper to taste
- 1/2 teaspoon Italian seasoning

- 1 tablespoon mayonnaise
- 2 fish fillets

Method:

1. Preheat your toaster oven to 425 degrees F.
2. Spray baking pan with oil.
3. In a bowl, mix the cheese, breadcrumbs, pepper and Italian seasoning.
4. Spread fish fillet with mayo.
5. Dredge with breadcrumb mixture.
6. Put the fish fillet in the baking pan.
7. Bake for 15 minutes.

Bagel Fish Fillets

Preparation Time: 10 minutes
Cooking Time: 10 minutes
Servings: 4

Ingredients:

- 4 white fish fillets
- 2 tbsp almond flour
- 1/4 cup bagel seasoning
- ing
- 1 tbsp mayonnaise
- 1 tsp lemon pepper season

Method:

1. In a small bowl, mix together bagel seasoning, almond flour, and lemon pepper seasoning.
2. Brush mayonnaise over fish fillets. Sprinkle seasoning mixture over fish fillets.
3. Place fish fillets on mesh rack then insert rack into the toaster oven.
4. Set the temperature to 400 F and timer for 10 minutes. Press start.
5. Serve and enjoy.

Healthy Salmon Patties

Preparation Time: 10 minutes
Cooking Time: 10 minutes
Servings: 4

Ingredients:

- 15 oz can salmon, drained and remove bones
- 1/4 cup onion, chopped
- 1 egg, lightly beaten
- 1 tsp dill, chopped
- 1/2 cup breadcrumbs
- Pepper
- Salt

Method:

1. Add all ingredients into the mixing bowl and mix until well combined.
2. Make patties from mixture and place on mesh rack then insert rack into the toaster oven.
3. Select air fry mode then set the temperature to 370 F and timer for 10 minutes. Press start. Turn patties halfway through.
4. Serve and enjoy.

Lemon Garlic Fish

Preparation Time: 10 minutes
Cooking Time: 10 minutes
Servings: 2

Ingredients:

- 12 oz white fish fillets
- 1/2 tsp garlic powder
- 1/2 tsp onion powder
- 1/2 tsp lemon pepper seasoning
- Pepper
- Salt

Method:

1. Spray fish fillets with cooking spray and season with onion powder, lemon pepper seasoning, garlic powder, pepper, and salt.
2. Place fish on mesh rack then insert rack into the toaster oven.
3. Select air fry mode then set the temperature to 360 F and timer for 6-10 minutes. Press start.
4. Serve and enjoy.

Spicy Scallops

Preparation Time: 10 minutes
Cooking Time: 4 minutes
Servings: 2

Ingredients:

- 8 scallops
- 1 tbsp olive oil
- ¼ tsp cayenne
- Pepper
- Salt

Method:

1. Brush scallops with oil and season with cayenne, pepper, and salt.
2. Place scallops on mesh rack then insert rack into the toaster oven.
3. Select air fry mode then set the temperature to 390 F and timer for 4 minutes. Press start.
4. Serve and enjoy.

Tuna Steaks

Preparation Time: 10 minutes
Cooking Time: 4 minutes
Servings: 2

Ingredients:

- 12 tuna steaks, skinless and boneless
- 1 tsp ginger, grated
- 4 tbsp soy sauce
- 1/2 tsp rice vinegar
- 1 tsp sesame oil

Method:

1. Add tuna steaks and remaining ingredients in the zip-lock bag. Seal bag and place in the refrigerator for 30 minutes.
2. Place tuna steaks on mesh rack then insert rack into the toaster oven.
3. Select air fry mode then set the temperature to 380 F and timer for 4 minutes. Press start.
4. Serve and enjoy.

Juicy Baked Cod

Preparation Time: 10 minutes
Cooking Time: 10 minutes
Servings:2

Ingredients:

- 1 lb cod fillets
- 1 tbsp lemon juice
- 1 1/2 tbsp olive oil
- 3 dashes cayenne pepper
- 1/4 tsp salt

Method:

1. In a small bowl, mix together olive oil, cayenne pepper, lemon juice, and salt.
2. Brush fish fillets with oil mixture.
3. Place fish fillets on mesh rack then insert rack into the toaster oven.
4. Set the temperature to 400 F and timer for 10 minutes. Press start.
5. Serve and enjoy.

Baked Sole & Asparagus

Preparation Time: 15 minutes
Cooking Time: 20 minutes
Servings: 2

Ingredients:

- Cooking spray
- 2 cups asparagus, trimmed and sliced
- 1 teaspoon olive oil
- Salt and pepper to taste
- 2 sole fillets
- Parmesan cheese, grated

Method:

1. Preheat toaster oven to 450 degrees F.
2. Spray baking pan with oil.
3. Put asparagus on one side.
4. Drizzle with oil and season with salt and pepper.
5. Add the sole fillets on the other side of the pan.
6. Brush with oil and sprinkle with salt and pepper.
7. Sprinkle with Parmesan cheese.
8. Bake for 15 to 20 minutes.

Broiled Salmon with Zucchini

Preparation Time: 15 minutes
Cooking Time: 15 minutes
Servings: 2

Ingredients:

- 2 salmon fillets
- 2 tablespoons olive oil, divided

- Salt and pepper to taste
- 1 zucchini, sliced

Method:

1. Set the toaster oven to broil.
2. Brush salmon with half of olive oil.
3. Season with salt and pepper.
4. Coat zucchini with remaining oil and sprinkle with salt and pepper.
5. Place zucchini and salmon in a baking pan.
6. Cook in the toaster oven for 10 to 15 minutes.

Chapter 5: Vegetable

Roasted Snap Peas

Preparation Time: 10 minutes

Cooking Time: 10 minutes

Servings: 2

Ingredients:

- 8 oz. sugar snap peas
- 2 teaspoons olive oil
- 1 tablespoon shallot, chopped
- Salt to taste
- 1/2 teaspoon Italian seasoning

Method:

1. Preheat your toaster oven to 400 degrees F.
2. Combine all ingredients in a bowl.
3. Transfer to a small baking pan.
4. Roast in the oven for 10 minutes.

Squash Mac & Cheese

Preparation Time: 15 minutes

Cooking Time: 30 minutes

Servings: 6

Ingredients:

- 8 oz. elbow macaroni
- 1 butternut squash, sliced into cubes and boiled

- 1 cup milk
- 1/4 cup Greek yogurt
- Pinch ground nutmeg
- Salt and pepper to taste
- 6 oz. cheddar cheese, shredded
- 1/2 cup Parmesan cheese, shredded
- 1/2 cup breadcrumbs

Method:

1. Cook elbow macaroni according to the directions in the package.
2. Drain and set aside.
3. Preheat your toaster oven to 400 degrees F.
4. Add squash, milk, yogurt, nutmeg, salt and pepper in a food processor.
5. Pulse until pureed.
6. Add to a pan over medium heat.
7. Stir in cheddar and Parmesan cheese.
8. Cook for 3 minutes.
9. Add pasta to a small baking pan.
10. Pour squash mixture on top.
11. Toss to coat evenly.
12. Sprinkle breadcrumbs on top.
13. Bake in the toaster oven for 20 minutes.

Paprika Cauliflower Bites

Preparation Time: 10 minutes
Cooking Time: 20 minutes
Servings: 4

Ingredients:

- 3 tablespoons olive oil
- 1 teaspoon paprika
- 1/8 teaspoon chili powder
- 1/4 teaspoon ground turmeric

- 1/2 teaspoon ground cumin
- Salt to taste
- 4 cups cauliflower florets

Method:

1. Preheat your toaster oven to 450 degrees F.
2. Combine oil with spices and salt.
3. Stir in cauliflower florets.
4. Coat evenly with mixture.
5. Pour into a small baking pan.
6. Roast for 20 minutes.

Baked Brussel Sprouts

Preparation Time: 10 minutes
Cooking Time: 40 minutes
Servings: 6

Ingredients:

- 1 ½ lb Brussels sprouts, cut ends & sliced in half
- 2 tbsp olive oil
- 1 lemon juice
- 1 tsp garlic powder
- Pepper
- Salt

Method:

1. In a bowl, toss Brussels sprouts with garlic powder, oil, pepper, and salt.
2. Add Brussels sprouts into the baking dish.
3. Place baking dish on mesh rack then insert rack into the toaster oven.
4. Set the temperature to 400 F and timer for 35-40 minutes. Press start.
5. Drizzle lemon juice over Brussels sprouts and serve.

Healthy Butternut Squash

Preparation Time: 10 minutes
Cooking Time: 40 minutes
Servings:4

Ingredients:

- 3 lbs butternut squash, peeled, seeded, and cut into 1-inch cubes
- 1 1/2 tbsp olive oil
- 1/2 tsp cinnamon
- 1 1/2 tbsp maple syrup
- Pepper
- Salt

Method:

1. In a mixing bowl, toss squash cubes with the remaining ingredients.
2. Spread squash cubes mesh rack then insert rack into the toaster oven.
3. Set the temperature to 400 F and timer for 35-40 minutes. Press start.
4. Serve and enjoy.

Sweet Potatoes & Apple

Preparation Time: 10 minutes
Cooking Time: 30 minutes
Servings: 2

Ingredients:

- 2 large green apples, diced
- 1 tbsp olive oil
- 2 tsp cinnamon
- 2 large sweet potatoes, diced
- 2 tbsp maple syrup

Method:

1. In a mixing bowl, toss sweet potatoes, apples, cinnamon, and oil.

2. Spread sweet potatoes and apples on mesh rack then insert rack into the toaster oven.
3. Set the temperature to 400 F and timer for 30 minutes. Press start.
4. Drizzle with maple syrup and serve.

Vegetable Casserole

Preparation Time: 15 minutes
Cooking Time: 25 minutes
Servings: 4

Ingredients:

- 2 teaspoons butter
- 1/4 cup breadcrumbs
- 2 tablespoons butter
- 1 1/2 cups milk
- 2 tablespoons all-purpose flour
- 1/2 cup Parmesan cheese, grated
- 3/4 cup cheddar cheese, shredded
- 16 oz. broccoli florets, steamed
- 16 oz. cauliflower florets, steamed

Method:

1. Preheat your toaster oven to 425 degrees F.
2. In a pan over medium heat, add 2 teaspoons butter and breadcrumbs. Cook for 3 minutes.
3. Transfer to a bowl. Set aside.
4. Add remaining butter to the pan.
5. Add milk, flour and cheeses.
6. Bring to a boil. Simmer for 3 minutes.
7. Turn off the stove.
8. Stir in veggies.
9. Pour mixture into a small baking pan.
10. Sprinkle buttered breadcrumbs on top.

11. Bake in the toaster oven for 15 minutes.

Curried Cauliflower Florets

Preparation Time: 10 minutes
Cooking Time: 15 minutes
Servings: 4

Ingredients:

- 2 lbs cauliflower, cut into florets
- 1 1/2 tsp curry powder
- 2 tsp fresh lemon juice
- 1 tbsp olive oil
- 1 tsp kosher salt

Method:

1. Toss cauliflower florets with curry powder, oil, and salt.
2. Spread cauliflower florets on mesh rack then insert rack into the toaster oven.
3. Set the temperature to 400 F and timer for 15 minutes. Press start.
4. Drizzle with lemon juice and serve.

Mushroom Casserole

Preparation Time: 15 minutes
Cooking Time: 35 minutes
Servings: 6

Ingredients:

- 14 oz. chicken broth
- 3 tablespoons cornstarch
- Salt and pepper to taste
- 1 tablespoon butter
- 1/4 cup onion, chopped
- 1 garlic clove, crushed and minced
- 12 oz. evaporated milk
- 3 cups cooked spaghetti

- 3 cups mushrooms
- 2 tablespoons Parmesan cheese, grated

Method:

1. Preheat your toaster oven to 350 degrees F.
2. In a bowl, mix chicken broth, cornstarch, salt and pepper.
3. Add butter to a pan over medium heat.
4. Cook onion and garlic for 3 minutes.
5. Stir in broth mixture
6. Bring to a boil and then simmer for 2 minutes.
7. Pour in milk, spaghetti and mushrooms.
8. Pour mixture to a small baking pan.
9. Bake for 20 minutes.
10. Sprinkle cheese on top.
11. Bake for 5 minutes.

Scalloped Potatoes

Preparation Time: 20 minutes
Cooking Time: 1 hour and 15 minutes
Servings: 6

Ingredients:

- 2 tablespoons butter
- 3 tablespoons all-purpose flour
- Salt and pepper to taste
- 1 1/2 cups milk
- 1/2 cup cheddar cheese, shredded
- 4 cups potatoes, sliced thinly
- 1 cup onion, sliced thinly

Method:

1. Preheat your toaster oven to 350 degrees F.

2. In a pan over medium heat, add butter and wait for it to melt.

3. Add flour and stir.

4. Sprinkle with salt and pepper.

5. Pour in milk.

6. Bring to a boil and then simmer for 2 minutes.

7. Stir in cheese.

8. Spray a small baking pan with oil.

9. Arrange the potatoes in the pan.

10. Layer with onion and cheese mixture.

11. Repeat layers.

12. Bake in the toaster oven for 1 hour.

Brussels Sprouts with Creamy Cheese Sauce

Preparation Time: 30 minutes

Cooking Time: 30 minutes

Servings: 6

Ingredients:

- 2 lb. Brussels sprouts
- 1 tablespoon olive oil
- Salt and pepper to taste
- 2 cloves garlic, chopped
- 3/4 cup sourdough bread, sliced into cubes
- 1 tablespoon fresh parsley, minced
- 1 tablespoon butter
- 1 cup all-purpose cream
- 1/8 teaspoon red pepper flakes
- 1/8 teaspoon ground nutmeg
- 1/2 cup cheddar cheese, shredded

Method:

1. Preheat your toaster oven to 450 degrees F.

2. Coat Brussels sprouts in oil, salt and pepper.

3. Place these in a baking pan.

4. Roast in the toaster oven for 10 minutes.

5. Add the garlic, bread, parsley and butter in a food processor.

6. Pulse until crumbly.

7. Stir in the remaining ingredients except cheese.

8. Spread mixture on top of Brussels sprouts.

9. Sprinkle cheese on top.

10. Reduce temperature to 400 degrees F.

11. Bake in the toaster oven for 20 minutes.

Buttered Cauliflower

Preparation Time: 15 minutes

Cooking Time: 55 minutes

Servings: 4

Ingredients:

- 6 cloves garlic
- 3 tablespoons butter
- 4 cups cauliflower florets
- Salt and pepper to taste
- 1/4 cup golden raisins
- 1/4 cup fresh parsley, chopped
- 1 tablespoon capers, chopped
- 2 teaspoons lemon juice

Method:

1. Preheat your toaster oven to 400 degrees F.

2. Wrap garlic cloves with foil.

3. Bake in the toaster oven for 30 minutes.

4. Peel garlic and mash. Set aside.

5. In a pan over medium heat, add butter and melt.

6. Arrange cauliflower in a small baking pan.

7. Drizzle with melted butter and season with salt and pepper.

8. Roast in the toaster oven for 20 minutes.

9. Transfer to a bowl.
10. Stir in garlic and the rest of ingredients.

Creamy Cauliflower

Preparation Time: 10 minutes
Cooking Time: 20 minutes
Servings: 4

Ingredients:

- 1 cauliflower head, cut into florets
- 1/2 cup mayonnaise
- 2 tsp Dijon mustard
- 1/4 cup sour cream
- 2 tbsp fresh lemon juice
- 1/2 cup cheddar cheese, shredded

Method:

1. Spread cauliflower florets on a roasting pan and bake for 10 minutes.
2. In a mixing bowl, stir together cauliflower, lemon juice, cheese, mayonnaise, mustard, and sour cream and pour into the baking dish.
3. Place baking dish on mesh rack then insert rack into the toaster oven.
4. Set the temperature to 375 F and timer for 20 minutes. Press start.
5. Serve and enjoy.

Broccoli Fritters

Preparation Time: 10 minutes
Cooking Time: 30 minutes
Servings: 4

Ingredients:

- 3 cups broccoli florets, cooked & chopped
- ¼ cup breadcrumbs
- 2 cups cheddar cheese, shredded

- 2 garlic cloves, minced
- 2 eggs, lightly beaten
- Pepper
- Salt

Method:

1. Add all ingredients into the large bowl and mix until well combined.
2. Make patties from mixture and place on mesh rack then insert rack into the toaster oven.
3. Set the temperature to 375 F and timer for 30 minutes. Press start.
4. Serve and enjoy.

Baked Carrots

Preparation Time: 10 minutes
Cooking Time: 30 minutes
Servings: 4

Ingredients:

- 24 baby carrots
- 1 tsp cinnamon
- 6 tbsp butter, melted
- 1/4 cup brown sugar
- Pepper
- Salt

Method:

1. Arrange baby carrots in the baking dish. Pour melted butter over baby carrots.
2. Sprinkle cinnamon, brown sugar, pepper, and salt over baby carrots.
3. Place baking dish on mesh rack then insert rack into the toaster oven.
4. Set the temperature to 390 F and timer for 25-30 minutes. Press start.
5. Serve and enjoy.

Easy Baked Potatoes

Preparation Time: 10 minutes

Cooking Time: 40 minutes

Servings: 4

Ingredients:

- 4 potatoes, scrubbed and washed
- ½ tbsp butter, melted
- ¾ tsp garlic powder
- ½ tsp Italian seasoning
- ½ tsp sea salt

Method:

1. Prick potatoes using a fork.
2. Rub potatoes with melted butter and sprinkle with garlic powder, Italian seasoning, and sea salt.
3. Arrange potatoes on mesh rack then insert rack into the toaster oven.
4. Set the temperature to 400 F and timer for 40 minutes. Press start.
5. Serve and enjoy.

Easy Zucchini Patties

Preparation Time: 10 minutes

Cooking Time: 25 minutes

Servings: 6

Ingredients:

- 1 egg, lightly beaten
- 1/4 cup parmesan cheese, grated
- 1/2 tbsp Dijon mustard
- 1/2 tbsp mayonnaise
- 1 cup zucchini, shredded
- 2 tbsp onion, minced
- 1/2 cup breadcrumbs
- Pepper
- Salt

Method:

1. Add all ingredients into the bowl and mix until well combined.

2. Make patties from the mixture and place on mesh rack then insert rack into the toaster oven.
3. Set the temperature to 400 F and timer for 25 minutes. Press start.
4. Serve and enjoy.

Veggie Stuffed Red Bell Peppers

Preparation Time: 30 minutes

Cooking Time: 1 hour

Servings: 6

Ingredients:

- 1 tablespoon olive oil
- 1 onion, chopped
- 1/4 green pepper, chopped
- 1 squash, chopped
- 1 zucchini, chopped
- 4 garlic cloves, crushed and minced
- 8 oz. tomato sauce
- 1 cup cooked white rice
- Salt to taste
- 1/2 cup mozzarella cheese
- 6 red bell peppers, tops sliced off and steamed
- 3 Provolone cheese slices

Method:

1. Preheat your toaster oven to 350 degrees F.
2. In a pan over medium heat, cook onion, green pepper and veggies in olive oil for 7 minutes.
3. Stir in garlic and spinach.
4. Cook for 1 minute.
5. Add tomato sauce, rice, salt and mozzarella cheese to the pan.
6. Stir and cook for 2 minutes.
7. Arrange red bell peppers in a small baking pan.
8. Stuff with the veggie mixture.

9. Bake for 40 minutes.
10. Put the provolone cheese on top.
11. Bake for 5 minutes.

Asparagus Strata

Preparation Time: 1 hour and 15 minutes
Cooking Time: 1 hour
Servings: 6

Ingredients:

- 5 eggs
- 1/2 cup cream
- 2 cups almond milk
- Pinch of ground nutmeg
- Salt and pepper to taste
- 4 cups Italian bread, sliced into cubes
- 1 cup asparagus, trimmed and sliced
- 1 1/4 cups Monterey Jack cheese

Method:

1. Beat eggs in a bowl.
2. Stir in the rest of the ingredients.
3. Pour mixture into a small baking pan.
4. Cover and refrigerate for 1 hour.
5. Preheat your toaster oven to 325 degrees F.
6. Bake for 20 minutes.
7. Cover with foil and bake for another 40 minutes.

Zucchini Bake

Preparation Time: 10 minutes

Cooking Time: 45 minutes

Servings: 6

Ingredients:

- 3 zucchini, grated
- 1/2 cup mozzarella cheese, shredded
- 1/2 cup feta cheese, crumbled
- 1/2 cup dill, chopped
- 3 tbsp butter, melted
- 1/2 cup flour
- 3 eggs, lightly beaten
- Pepper
- Salt

Method:

1. In a mixing bowl, mix together zucchini, cheeses, dill, eggs, butter, pepper, flour, and salt.
2. Pour the zucchini mixture into the baking dish.
3. Place baking dish on mesh rack then insert rack into the toaster oven.
4. Set the temperature to 350 F and timer for 45 minutes. Press start.
5. Serve and enjoy.

Chapter 6: Snack / Appetizer

Parmesan-Crusted Peas

Preparation Time: 15 minutes
Cooking Time: 15 minutes
Servings: 4

Ingredients:

- 1 clove garlic, crushed and minced
- 3 tablespoons olive oil
- 2 cups peas
- 1/2 cup Parmesan cheese, shredded

Method:

1. Preheat your toaster oven to 350 degrees F.
2. Toss garlic in oil.
3. Place in a small baking pan.
4. Bake in the toaster oven for 5 minutes.
5. Stir in peas.
6. Bake for 10 minutes.
7. Sprinkle with Parmesan cheese.

Bruschetta

Preparation Time: 15 minutes
Cooking Time: 5 minutes
Servings: 6

Ingredients:

- 4 cups fresh basil leaves
- 3 cloves garlic
- 1/2 cup pine nuts
- 1/2 cup Parmesan cheese
- 2 tablespoons balsamic vinegar
- 1 Italian bread loaf, sliced
- 2 tomatoes, chopped
- Salt and pepper to taste

Method:

1. Add basil, garlic, pine nuts, Parmesan cheese and vinegar to a food processor.
2. Pulse until smooth.
3. Spread basil mixture on top of the bread slices.
4. Top with the chopped tomatoes.
5. Sprinkle with salt and pepper.
6. Toast in the toaster oven for 5 minutes.

Yogurt Cornbread

Preparation Time: 20 minutes
Cooking Time: 30 minutes
Servings: 8

Ingredients:

- 1/4 cup all-purpose flour
- 1 cup yellow cornmeal
- 2 teaspoons baking powder
- 1/4 teaspoon baking soda
- Pinch salt
- 1 egg, beaten
- 1/2 cup milk
- 1 cup yogurt
- 1 tablespoon honey
- 1/4 cup oil

Method:

1. In a bowl, mix the flour, cornmeal, baking powder, baking soda and salt.
2. In another bowl, combine the remaining ingredients.

3. Add the second bowl to the first one. Mix well.
4. Pour into a small baking pan.
5. Bake in the toaster oven at 350 degrees F for 20 to 30 minutes.

Chicken Nachos

Preparation Time: 15 minutes
Cooking Time: 30 minutes
Servings: 4

Ingredients:

- Cooking spray
- Tortilla chips
- 2 cups chicken, cooked and shredded
- 2 cups salsa, divided
- 2 cups Monterey Jack cheese, shredded and divided
- 1 fresh jalapeno, sliced
- 1 cup black beans, rinsed and drained

Method:

1. Preheat toaster oven to 350 degrees F.
2. Spray small baking pan with oil.
3. Arrange the chips in the baking pan.
4. Top with the remaining ingredients, reserving 1 cup salsa for dip and 1 cup cheese for topping.
5. Bake in the toaster oven for 20 minutes.
6. Sprinkle cheese on top and bake for another 10 minutes.
7. Serve with reserved salsa.

Tasty Ranch Chickpeas

Preparation Time: 10 minutes

Cooking Time: 12 minutes

Servings: 4

Ingredients:

- 14.5 oz can chickpeas, rinsed, drained and pat dry
- 1 1/2 tsp ranch seasoning
- Pepper
- Salt

Method:

1. Add chickpeas, ranch seasoning, pepper, and salt into the mixing bowl and toss well.
2. Spread chickpeas on mesh rack then insert rack into the toaster oven.
3. Select toaster mode then set the temperature to 375 F and timer for 12 minutes. Press start. Stir halfway through.
4. Serve and enjoy.

Mexican Cheese Dip

Preparation Time: 10 minutes

Cooking Time: 30 minutes

Servings: 10

Ingredients:

- 16 oz cream cheese, softened
- 3 cups cheddar cheese, shredded
- 1 cup sour cream
- 1/2 cup salsa

Method:

1. In a mixing bowl, mix together all ingredients until well combined and pour into the baking dish.
2. Place a baking dish on a mesh rack then insert the rack into the toaster oven.
3. Set the temperature to 350 F and timer for 30 minutes. Press start.
4. Serve and enjoy.

Flavorful Potato Wedges

Preparation Time: 10 minutes
Cooking Time: 24 minutes
Servings: 2

Ingredients:

- 1/2 lb potatoes, cut into wedges
- ¼ tsp chili powder
- 1 tbsp olive oil
- Pepper
- Salt

Method:

1. In a bowl, toss potato wedges with oil, chili powder, pepper, and salt.
2. Place Potato wedges on mesh rack then insert rack into the toaster oven.
3. Select toaster mode then set the temperature to 390 F and timer for 24 minutes. Press start. Stir halfway through.
4. Serve and enjoy.

Zucchini Bites

Preparation Time: 10 minutes
Cooking Time: 10 minutes
Servings: 4

Ingredients:

- 1 cup breadcrumbs
- 1 egg, lightly beaten
- 4 zucchini, grated
- 1 tsp Italian seasoning
- 1/2 cup parmesan cheese, grated

Method:

1. Add all ingredients into the bowl and mix until well combined.

2. Make small balls from the zucchini mixture and place on mesh rack then insert rack into the toaster oven.
3. Select toaster mode then set the temperature to 400 F and timer for 10 minutes. Press start.
4. Serve and enjoy.

Roasted Pumpkin Seeds

Preparation Time: 5 minutes
Cooking Time: 50 minutes
Servings: 4

Ingredients:

- 4 cups pumpkin seeds
- 1 tablespoon olive oil
- Salt to taste

Method:

1. Preheat your toaster oven to 300 degrees F.
2. Spread pumpkin seeds on a small baking pan.
3. Roast in the toaster oven for 30 minutes.
4. Coat seeds with olive oil and season with salt.
5. Roast for another 20 minutes.

Broccoli Pop-corn

Preparation Time: 10 minutes
Cooking Time: 6 minutes
Servings: 4

Ingredients:

- 4 eggs yolks
- 2 cups broccoli florets
- 2 cups coconut flour
- Pepper
- Salt

Method:

1. In a small bowl, whisk eggs with pepper and salt.
2. In a shallow dish, add coconut flour.
3. Dip broccoli floret with egg and coat with coconut flour and place on mesh rack then insert rack into the toaster oven.
4. Select toaster mode then set the temperature to 400 F and timer for 6 minutes. Press start.
5. Serve and enjoy.

Spicy Cheese Dip

Preparation Time: 10 minutes
Cooking Time: 20 minutes
Servings: 14

Ingredients:

- 8.5 oz can green chilies
- ¼ tsp cumin
- 1 tsp garlic, minced
- 15 oz cream cheese, softened
- ¼ tsp pepper
- 2 cups cheddar cheese, shredded
- ¼ tsp salt

Method:

1. Add all ingredients into the mixing bowl and mix until well combined.
2. Pour mixture into the baking dish.
3. Place a baking dish on a mesh rack then insert the rack into the toaster oven.
4. Set the temperature to 350 F and timer for 20 minutes. Press start.
5. Serve and enjoy.

Corn Dip

Preparation Time: 10 minutes
Cooking Time: 20 minutes
Servings: 6

Ingredients:

- 15 oz can corn kernel, drained
- ½ cup cheddar cheese, shredded
- 1 tsp smoked paprika
- ¼ cup sour cream
- 1 tbsp green chilies, diced
- 2 green onions, sliced
- ½ bell pepper, diced
- 1/3 cup mayonnaise

Method:

1. Add all ingredients into the mixing bowl and mix until well combined.
2. Pour mixture into the baking dish.
3. Place a baking dish on a mesh rack then insert the rack into the toaster oven.
4. Set the temperature to 350 F and timer for 20 minutes. Press start.
5. Serve with enjoy.

Maple Chickpeas

Preparation Time: 10 minutes
Cooking Time: 12 minutes
Servings: 4

Ingredients:

- 14 oz can chickpeas, rinsed, drained and pat dry
- 1 tbsp maple syrup
- 1 tbsp olive oil
- 1 tsp ground cinnamon
- 1 tbsp brown sugar
- Pepper
- Salt

Method:

1. Spread chickpeas on mesh rack then insert rack into the toaster oven.
2. Select toaster mode then set the temperature to 375 F and timer for 12 minutes. Press start. Stir halfway through.
3. In a mixing bowl, mix together cinnamon, brown sugar, maple syrup, oil, pepper, and salt. Add chickpeas and toss well to coat.
4. Serve and enjoy.

Asparagus Fries

Preparation Time: 15 minutes

Cooking Time: 15 minutes

Servings: 4

Ingredients:

- 1 1/2 cups mayonnaise
- 2 cloves garlic, crushed and minced
- 3/4 cup Parmesan cheese, grated
- 1 tablespoon Italian seasoning
- 1 tablespoon dried parsley
- Salt and pepper to taste
- 1/2 lb. thick asparagus, trimmed
- 1 cup breadcrumbs

Method:

1. Preheat your toaster oven to 425 degrees F.
2. In a bowl, mix the mayo, garlic, Parmesan cheese, Italian seasoning, parsley, salt and pepper.
3. Take 1 cup of the mixture and reserve for later.
4. Coat the asparagus with the remaining mayo mixture and then dredge with breadcrumbs.
5. Arrange on a small baking pan.
6. Bake for 15 minutes.
7. Serve with reserved mayo dip.

Healthy Cashew Nuts

Preparation Time: 10 minutes
Cooking Time: 5 minutes
Servings: 6

Ingredients:

- 3 cups cashews
- 1 tsp ground coriander
- 1 tsp paprika
- 2 tbsp olive oil
- 1 tsp ground cumin
- 1 tsp salt

Method:

1. Add cashews and remaining ingredients into the mixing bowl and toss well.
2. Spread cashews on mesh rack then insert rack into the toaster oven.
3. Select toaster mode then set the temperature to 330 F and timer for 5 minutes. Press start. Stir halfway through.
4. Serve and enjoy.

Vegetable Fritters

Preparation Time: 10 minutes
Cooking Time: 15 minutes
Servings: 2

Ingredients:

- 1 egg, lightly beaten
- 1 1/2 cups frozen vegetable, cooked & mashed
- 1/2 tbsp coconut flour
- 1/4 tsp garlic powder
- 1/4 cup parmesan cheese, shredded
- Pepper
- Salt

Method:

1. Add mash vegetables and egg in a bowl and mix well.
2. Add parmesan cheese, coconut flour, garlic powder, pepper, and salt and stir well.
3. Make patties from the mixture and place on mesh rack then insert rack into the toaster oven.
4. Select toaster mode then set the temperature to 390 F and timer for 15 minutes. Press start.
5. Serve and enjoy.

Spicy Lime Chickpeas

Preparation Time: 10 minutes
Cooking Time: 12 minutes
Servings:4

Ingredients:

- 14 oz can chickpeas, rinsed, drained and pat dry
- 1/2 tsp chili powder
- 1 tbsp olive oil
- 1 tbsp lime juice
- 1/4 tsp red pepper
- Pepper
- Salt

Method:

1. Add chickpeas, red pepper, chili powder, oil, pepper, and salt into the mixing bowl and toss well.
2. Place chickpeas on mesh rack then insert rack into the toaster oven.
3. Select toaster mode then set the temperature to 375 F and timer for 12 minutes. Press start. Stir halfway through.
4. Drizzle lemon juice over chickpeas and serve.

Pepperoni Bites

Preparation Time: 15 minutes

Cooking Time: 10 minutes

Servings: 8

Ingredients:

- 8 oz. crescent rolls, sliced
- 16 pepperoni slices
- 2 oz. string cheese, sliced
- Garlic salt to taste

Method:

1. Unroll the dough.
2. Add pepperoni slices and cheese on top.
3. Season with garlic salt.
4. Roll them up.
5. Bake in the toaster oven at 375 degrees F for 10 minutes.

Simple French Fries

Preparation Time: 10 minutes
Cooking Time: 15 minutes
Servings: 4

Ingredients:

- 2 potatoes, peel & cut into fries shape
- 1/2 tbsp olive oil
- 1/2 tsp garlic powder
- Pepper
- Salt

Method:

1. Soak potato fries in water for 15 minutes. Drain well and pat dry with a paper towel.
2. Toss potato fries with oil, garlic powder, pepper, and salt.
3. Spread potato fries on mesh rack then insert rack into the toaster oven.

4. Select toaster mode then set the temperature to 375 F and timer for 15 minutes. Press start. Stir halfway through.
5. Serve and enjoy.

Lentil Loaf

Preparation Time: 30 minutes
Cooking Time: 1 hour and 40 minutes
Servings: 6

Ingredients:

- 14 oz. vegetable broth
- 3/4 cup brown lentils, rinsed and drained
- Cooking spray
- 1 tablespoon olive oil
- 1 cup onion, chopped
- 1 cup mushrooms, chopped
- 2 cups carrots, shredded
- 1 tablespoon fresh parsley, minced
- 2 tablespoons fresh basil, minced
- 1 cup mozzarella, shredded
- 1/2 cup cooked brown rice
- 1 egg
- 1 egg white
- Salt and pepper to taste
- 1/2 teaspoon garlic powder
- 2 tablespoons tomato paste
- 2 tablespoons water

Method:

1. Pour broth into a pot over medium heat.
2. Add lentil and bring to a boil.
3. Reduce heat and simmer for 30 minutes.
4. Drain and set aside.
5. Preheat your toaster oven to 350 degrees F.
6. Spray your loaf pan with oil.
7. In a pan over medium heat, cook onion, mushrooms and carrots for 10 minutes.
8. Season with herbs.

9. Transfer to a bowl.
10. Stir in the rest of the ingredients along with the cooked lentils.
11. Mix and pour mixture into the loaf pan.
12. Bake in the toaster oven for 50 minutes.

Spicy Peanuts

Preparation Time: 10 minutes
Cooking Time: 10 minutes
Servings: 4

Ingredients:

- 1 cup peanuts
- ¼ tsp chili powder
- 2 tbsp olive oil
- Salt

Method:

1. In a bowl, toss peanuts, oil, chili powder, and salt.
2. Place peanuts on mesh rack then insert rack into the toaster oven.
3. Select toaster mode then set the temperature to 320 F and timer for 10 minutes. Press start. Stir halfway through.

Ricotta Cheese Dip

Preparation Time: 10 minutes
Cooking Time: 20 minutes
Servings: 6

Ingredients:

- 2 cups ricotta cheese
- 2 tsp fresh thyme, chopped
- 1 lemon zest
- ¼ cup parmesan cheese, shredded
- ½ cup mozzarella cheese, shredded
- 3 tbsp olive oil

- 2 garlic cloves, minced
- Pepper
- Salt

Method:

1. Add all ingredients into the bowl and mix until well combined.
2. Pour mixture into the baking dish.
3. Place a baking dish on a mesh rack then insert the rack into the toaster oven.
4. Set the temperature to 375 F and timer for 20 minutes. Press start.
5. Serve and enjoy.

Cajun Okra

Preparation Time: 15 minutes
Cooking Time: 40 minutes
Servings: 4

Ingredients:

- Cooking spray
- 1 lb. okra, sliced lengthwise
- 1 teaspoon Cajun seasoning
- 2 tablespoons olive oil
- Salt and pepper to taste

Method:

1. Preheat your toaster oven to 450 degrees F.
2. Spray a small baking pan with oil.
3. Combine all the ingredients in the baking pan.
4. Coat evenly with the mixture.
5. Bake in the toaster oven for 40 minutes.

Baked Sweet Potatoes

Preparation Time: 20 minutes
Cooking Time: 1 hour and 30 minutes
Servings: 6

Ingredients:

- 6 sweet potatoes
- 2 tablespoons butter
- Garlic powder to taste
- 1 tablespoon fresh parsley, chopped

Method:

1. Preheat your toaster oven to 450 degrees F.
2. Poke the sweet potatoes with fork.
3. Place sweet potatoes in a small baking pan.
4. Bake for 1 hour.
5. Brush with butter and sprinkle with garlic powder and parsley.
6. Bake for another 30 minutes.

Carrot Fries

Preparation Time: 10 minutes
Cooking Time: 15 minutes
Servings:4

Ingredients:

- 4 carrots, peeled and cut into fries
- 2 tbsp olive oil
- 2 tbsp parmesan cheese, grated
- 1 1/2 tbsp garlic, minced
- Pepper
- Salt

Method:

1. Add carrots and remaining ingredients into the mixing bowl and toss well.
2. Place carrot fries on mesh rack then insert rack into the toaster oven.
3. Select toaster mode then set the temperature to 350 F and timer for 15 minutes. Press start. Stir halfway through.
4. Serve and enjoy.

Chapter 7: Dessert

Peanut Butter Cookies

Preparation Time: 20 minutes

Cooking Time: 20 minutes

Servings: 4

Ingredients:

- 1 1/2 cups all-purpose flour
- 1 teaspoon baking soda
- 1/2 cup peanut butter
- 1/2 cup vegetable shortening
- 1 egg, beaten
- 1 1/4 cups brown sugar
- 1 teaspoon vanilla
- Pinch salt

Method:

1. Preheat your toaster oven to 275 degrees F.
2. Combine all the ingredients in a bowl.
3. Mix well.
4. Form cookies from the mixture and place in a small cookie sheet.
5. Bake for 20 minutes.

Peach Cobbler

Preparation Time: 20 minutes

Cooking Time: 45 minutes

Servings: 8

Ingredients:

- 1/4 cup cornstarch
- 1/2 cup brown sugar
- 2 tablespoons lemon juice
- 8 peaches, sliced in half
- 1 1/4 cups all-purpose flour
- 1 teaspoon ginger, grated
- 1 teaspoon lemon zest
- 1/2 cup sugar
- 3 tablespoons milk
- 1/2 cup melted butter
- Salt to taste

Method:

1. Preheat your toaster oven to 350 degrees F.
2. Mix the cornstarch, brown sugar and lemon juice in a bowl.
3. Coat peaches with this mixture and place on a small baking dish.
4. In another bowl, mix the remaining ingredients.
5. Pour mixture on top of the peaches.
6. Bake for 45 minutes.

Chocolate Cake

Preparation Time: 10 minutes
Cooking Time: 25 minutes
Servings: 8

Ingredients:

- 1 egg
- 3 tbsp cocoa powder
- 1 cup of sugar
- 1 cup all-purpose flour
- 1 tsp baking soda
- 1 tsp baking powder
- 1 tsp vanilla
- 1/4 cup butter
- 1 cup boiling water
- 1/4 tsp salt

Method:

1. Spray a baking dish with cooking spray and set aside.
2. Add butter and boiling water in a bowl and beat until butter is melted.

3. Add vanilla and egg and beat until well combined.
4. In a medium bowl, mix together flour, baking soda, baking powder, cocoa powder, sugar, and salt.
5. Add egg mixture into the flour mixture and beat until well combined.
6. Pour batter into prepared baking dish.
7. Place a baking dish on a mesh rack then insert the rack into the toaster oven.
8. Set the temperature to 350 F and timer for 25 minutes. Press start.
9. Serve and enjoy.

Simple Vanilla Muffins

Preparation Time: 10 minutes
Cooking Time: 20 minutes
Servings: 12

Ingredients:

- 3 eggs
- 1/2 cup butter
- 2/3 cup sugar
- 1 1/2 tsp baking powder
- 1/4 cup milk
- 1 tsp vanilla
- 1 1/2 cups all-purpose flour
- 1/4 tsp salt

Method:

1. Line the muffin pan with cupcake liners and set aside.
2. In a bowl, mix flour, salt, and baking powder and set aside.
3. In a separate bowl, beat the sugar and butter until fluffy.
4. Add eggs one by one and beat until well combined.
5. Add flour mixture and beat until well combined.
6. Add milk, vanilla, and remaining flour mixture and beat until completely incorporated.
7. Pour mixture into the prepared muffin pan.
8. Place muffin pan on mesh rack then insert rack into the toaster oven.
9. Set the temperature to 350 F and timer for 20 minutes. Press start.
10. Serve and enjoy.

Baked Spiced Apples

Preparation Time: 10 minutes
Cooking Time: 10 minutes
Servings:4

Ingredients:

- 4 apples, sliced
- 2 tbsp butter, melted
- 1 tsp apple pie spice
- 2 tbsp sugar

Method:

1. Add apple slices into the mixing bowl. Add remaining ingredients on top of apple slices and toss until well coated.
2. Place apple slices in a baking pan.
3. Place baking pan on mesh rack then insert rack into the toaster oven..
4. Set the temperature to 350 F and timer for 10 minutes. Press start.
5. Serve and enjoy.

Easy Baked Donuts

Preparation Time: 10 minutes
Cooking Time: 8 minutes
Servings:6

Ingredients:

- 2 eggs
- 1/4 tsp cinnamon
- 1/4 tsp nutmeg
- 2 tsp baking powder
- 3/4 cup sugar
- 2 tbsp butter, melted
- 1 tsp vanilla
- 3/4 cup buttermilk
- 2 cups flour
- 1 tsp salt

Method:

1. In a bowl, whisk eggs, butter, vanilla, and buttermilk until well combined.
2. In a large bowl, mix together flour, cinnamon, nutmeg, baking powder, sugar, and salt.
3. Pour egg mixture into the flour mixture and mix until well combined.
4. Pour batter into the 6 silicone donut molds.
5. Place donut molds on mesh rack then insert rack into the toaster oven..
6. Set the temperature to 325 F and timer for 8 minutes. Press start.
7. Serve and enjoy.

Baked Blueberry Donuts

Preparation Time: 10 minutes
Cooking Time: 10 minutes
Servings: 6

Ingredients:

- 1 egg
- 3 tbsp yogurt
- 1/2 tsp vanilla
- 3 tbsp butter, melted
- 1/4 cup blueberries
- 1/4 cup milk
- 1/3 cup sugar
- 1/4 tsp baking soda
- 3/4 tsp baking powder
- 1 cup flour
- Pinch of salt

Method:

1. In a bowl, mix together flour, sugar, baking soda, baking powder, and salt.
2. In a separate bowl, whisk an egg with butter, vanilla, yogurt, and milk until smooth.
3. Pour wet ingredients mixture into the flour mixture and mix until smooth.
4. Add blueberries and stir well.
5. Pour batter into the 6 silicone donut molds.
6. Place donut molds on mesh rack then insert rack into the toaster oven.
7. Set the temperature to 350 F and timer for 10 minutes. Press start.
8. Serve and enjoy.

Choco Chip Cookies

Preparation Time: 20 minutes
Cooking Time: 15 minutes
Servings: 16

Ingredients:

- 1 1/2 cups all-purpose flour
- 1 teaspoon baking powder
- 1 egg
- 1 tablespoon milk
- 1/2 cup shortening
- 1/4 cup granulated sugar
- 1/2 cup brown sugar
- Pinch salt
- 1 cup chocolate chips

Method:

1. Preheat your toaster oven to 375 degrees F.
2. Combine all ingredients except chocolate chips in a bowl.
3. Use a mixer to beat ingredients on medium speed.
4. Fold in chocolate chips.
5. Form cookies from the mixture and arrange on a small cookie pan.
6. Bake for 10 to 15 minutes.

Lemon Muffins

Preparation Time: 10 minutes
Cooking Time: 20 minutes
Servings: 12

Ingredients:

- 1 egg
- 1 tsp vanilla
- 1 cup Greek yogurt
- 1/3 cup butter, melted

- 1/3 cup fresh lemon juice
- 2 tbsp lemon zest
- ¾ tsp baking soda
- 1 tsp baking powder
- ½ cup sugar
- 1 ¾ cups all-purpose flour
- ¼ tsp salt

Method:

1. Line 12-cup muffin pan with cupcake liners and set aside.
2. Add all dry ingredients into the mixing bowl and mix until well combined.
3. In a separate bowl, mix all wet ingredients. Add dry ingredient mixture into the wet ingredient mixture and mix until combined.
4. Spoon batter into the prepared muffin pan.
5. Place muffin pan on mesh rack then insert rack into the toaster oven..
6. Set the temperature to 400 F and timer for 20 minutes. Press start.
7. Serve and enjoy.

Moist Peanut Butter Muffins

Preparation Time: 10 minutes
Cooking Time: 20 minutes
Servings: 12

Ingredients:

- 1 egg
- 1 1/2 tsp vanilla
- 2 1/2 tsp baking powder
- 2/3 cup brown sugar
- 1 3/4 cups flour
- 1/4 cup oil
- 2/3 cup peanut butter
- 3/4 cup milk
- 1/4 tsp salt

Method:

1. In a bowl, mix together flour, baking powder, brown sugar, and salt.
2. In a small bowl, whisk egg, vanilla, oil, peanut butter, and milk.
3. Pour egg mixture into the flour mixture and mix until well combined.

4. Pour batter into the 12 silicone muffin molds.
5. Place muffin molds on mesh rack then insert rack into the toaster oven..
6. Set the temperature to 350 F and timer for 20 minutes. Press start.
7. Serve and enjoy.

Sweetened Grapefruit

Preparation Time: 5 minutes
Cooking Time: 5 minutes
Servings: 2

Ingredients:

- 2 teaspoons brown sugar
- 2 tablespoons granulated sugar
- 1 grapefruit, sliced in half
- Pinch salt

Method:

1. In a bowl, mix the 2 sugars.
2. Sprinkle on top of the grapefruit.
3. Set your toaster oven to broil.
4. Broil the grapefruit for 5 minutes.
5. Sprinkle with salt and serve.

Blueberry Loaf Cake

Preparation Time: 20 minutes
Cooking Time: 1 hour and 20 minutes
Servings: 5

Ingredients:

- Cooking spray
- Vegetable oil
- 2 cups all-purpose flour
- 3/4 cup white sugar
- 2 teaspoons lemon zest
- 1 1/2 teaspoons baking powder
- 1/4 teaspoon salt
- 2 eggs, beaten
- 1/2 cup melted butter
- 1/2 cup milk
- 1 cup blueberries
- 1/2 cup walnuts, chopped

Method:

1. Preheat your toaster oven to 350 degrees F.
2. Grease your loaf pan with oil.
3. Combine all the ingredients in a bowl.
4. Pour into the loaf pan.
5. Bake in the toaster oven for 1 hour and 20 minutes.

Brownie Cookies

Preparation Time: 20 minutes

Cooking Time: 10 minutes

Servings: 6

Ingredients:

- 1 1/2 cups light brown sugar
- 2/3 cup shortening
- 2 eggs, beaten
- 1 teaspoon vanilla
- 1 tablespoon water
- 1 1/4 cups all-purpose flour
- 1/4 teaspoon baking soda
- 1/3 cup unsweetened baking cocoa
- 12 oz. chocolate chips
- Pinch salt

Method:

1. Preheat your toaster oven to 375 degrees F.

2. In a bowl, mix brown sugar and shortening.
3. Stir in eggs, vanilla and water.
4. Slowly add the remaining ingredients.
5. Form cookies from the mixture.
6. Bake for 10 minutes.

Delicious Brownies

Preparation Time: 10 minutes
Cooking Time: 30 minutes
Servings: 6

Ingredients:

- 2 eggs
- 1 cup brown sugar
- 2 tsp vanilla
- 1/4 cup cocoa powder
- 1/2 cup butter, melted
- 1/2 cup walnuts, chopped
- 1/4 cup all-purpose flour
- 1/8 tsp salt

Method:

1. Spray a baking dish with cooking spray and set aside.
2. In a bowl, whisk eggs with vanilla, butter, and cocoa powder.
3. Add flour, walnuts, sugar, and salt and stir until well combined.
4. Pour batter into the prepared baking dish.
5. Place a baking dish on a mesh rack then insert the rack into the toaster oven.
6. Set the temperature to 320 F and timer for 30 minutes. Press start.
7. Serve and enjoy.

Brownie Muffins

Preparation Time: 10 minutes
Cooking Time: 15 minutes

Servings: 6

Ingredients:

- 3 eggs
- 1/2 cup Swerve
- 1 cup almond flour
- 1 tbsp gelatin
- 1/3 cup butter, melted
- 1/3 cup cocoa powder

Method:

1. Line the muffin pan with cupcake liners and set aside.
2. Add all ingredients into the bowl and stir until just combined.
3. Pour batter into the prepared muffin pan.
4. Place muffin pan on mesh rack then insert rack into the toaster oven..
5. Set the temperature to 350 F and timer for 15 minutes. Press start.
6. Serve and enjoy.

Donuts

Preparation Time: 20 minutes
Cooking Time: 15 minutes
Servings: 6

Ingredients:

- 1 cup all-purpose flour
- 1/3 cup granulated sugar
- 1 1/2 teaspoons baking powder
- 2 tablespoons melted butter
- 1/2 cup buttermilk
- 1 egg
- 1 tablespoon vanilla extract
- Pinch of salt

Method:

1. Preheat your toaster oven to 350 degrees F.
2. In a bowl, combine all the ingredients.

3. Pour mixture into a donut pan.

4. Bake for 15 to 20 minutes.

Apple & Carrot Muffins

Preparation Time: 30 minutes
Cooking Time: 30 minutes
Servings: 10

Ingredients:

- 2 cups all-purpose flour
- 1 1/2 teaspoons baking powder
- 1/4 cup oil
- 1 cup milk
- 4 carrots, grated
- 1 apple, grated
- 1/2 cup applesauce
- 3 eggs, beaten
- 1/4 cup white sugar
- 2 teaspoons cinnamon powder
- 1 teaspoon vanilla extract
- Pinch salt

Method:

1. Combine all the ingredients in a bowl.

2. Pour mixture into a muffin pan.

3. Bake in the toaster oven at 400 degrees F for 25 to 30 minutes.

Lemon Brownies

Preparation Time: 10 minutes
Cooking Time: 20 minutes
Servings: 16

Ingredients:

- 2 eggs
- ¾ cup all-purpose flour
- 1 tbsp fresh lemon juice
- ½ tsp baking powder

- ½ lemon zest
- ¾ cup sugar
- ½ cup butter, softened

Method:

1. In a large bowl, beat sugar, butter, and lemon zest until fluffy.
2. Add eggs, lemon juice, and flour and mix until combined.
3. Pour batter into the greased baking pan and spread evenly.
4. Place the pan on a mesh rack then insert the rack into the toaster oven.
5. Set the temperature to 350 F and timer for 20 minutes. Press start.
6. Serve and enjoy.

Chocolate & Vanilla Cookies

Preparation Time: 20 minutes

Cooking Time: 15 minutes

Servings: 6

Ingredients:

- 2 cups all-purpose flour
- 2 cups rolled oats
- 1 cup butter
- 2 eggs
- 1 cup brown sugar
- 1 cup sugar

- ½ teaspoon baking powder
- 1 teaspoon baking soda
- ½ teaspoon salt
- 1 tablespoon vanilla
- 12 oz. chocolate chips

Method:

1. Preheat your toaster oven to 350 degrees F.
2. Combine all the ingredients in a bowl.

3. Form cookies from the mixture.

4. Arrange on a small cookie sheet.

5. Bake in the toaster oven for 15 minutes.

Mug Cake

Preparation Time: 20 minutes

Cooking Time: 20 minutes

Serving: 1

Ingredients:

- 1/4 cup all-purpose flour
- 1/4 teaspoon baking powder
- 1/8 teaspoon baking soda
- 2 tablespoons sugar
- Pinch of salt
- 2 tablespoons applesauce
- 2 tablespoons milk
- 1/2 tablespoon vegetable oil
- 1/4 teaspoon vanilla extract
- 2 tablespoons chocolate chips

Method:

1. Preheat your toaster oven to 375 degrees F.

2. Mix the flour, baking powder, baking soda, sugar and salt in a bowl.

3. In another bowl, combine the remaining ingredients.

4. Slowly add second bowl to the first one.

5. Mix well.

6. Pour into an oven-safe mug.

7. Bake for 15 to 20 minutes.

CPSIA information can be obtained
at www.ICGtesting.com
Printed in the USA
LVHW111402121121
703156LV00004B/25

9 781954 703513